THE FIRST 95 YEARS

KEN FORD

H BAR PRESS

CONTENTS

Ken, Yosemite National Park, California, 1955

PREFACE

This is not a memoir—not really my life story. It is a set of 26 essays of variable length—most pretty short—on bits and pieces of my life. It is episodic and anecdotal. Big chunks of my life, really the most important chunks, are left out—the joys of helping to raise children, having fun with them, spending time in Shunk, Pennsylvania, traveling the world, finding deep rewards in friendships, in research, and in marriage.

Despite its limitations, I hope this book will be of some interest to my children and grandchildren who want to know me a little better and to those who come later and might be curious about this particular ancestor. I myself am surprised by some of myself.

Original versions of some of these essays were written as assignments in three evening courses that I took in 2000, 2004, and 2007 (at ages 73, 77, and 80). Some were written more recently, as I crept up toward 95. The book's title is accurate as of May 1, 2021.

Two of my books are, in part, also autobiographical: *In Love with Flying* (which covers fifty years, ages 27 to 77), and *Building the H Bomb: A Personal History* (which covers two years, ages 24 to 26). In these essays I have avoided duplicating what is in those books.

* * * * *

In setting down these miscellaneous essays, my purpose has not been to highlight achievements. Instead I wanted to reveal something about my own character—what sort of person I am—and to make clear the good fortune that has relentlessly followed me in family, jobs, and experiences. Yes, good fortune, amazing good fortune, although I have reason enough for regret, too—for giving up prematurely on a first marriage, for tugging my wife Joanne hither and yon around the country when she would have happily stayed in one place, and for not figuring out how to succeed as a college president.

The essays also shed a bit of light on the times I lived through, notably the final two-thirds of the twentieth century, with all of its social and technological revolutions.

Since the essays are not organized according to a time line, let me here set forth a few dates. I was born in 1926 and turn 95 in 2021. I graduated from Exeter in 1944, served in the Navy from 1944 to 1946, graduated from Harvard in 1948, and received a Ph.D. from Princeton in 1953. I married Karin in 1953 when she was 19 and I was 27. We were divorced in 1961. I married Joanne in 1962

Ken, Shunk, Pennsylvania, September 9, 2019

when she was 29 and I was 36, and here we are, generally happy and harmonious, 58 years later. Paul was born in 1957 in Los Alamos, New Mexico; Sarah in 1958 in Waltham, Massachusetts; Nina in Boston, Massachusetts in 1959; Caroline in Boston in 1963; Adam in Boston in 1964; Jason in Costa Mesa, California in 1966; and Lucas (now Star) in Los Alamos in 1968. The first of our thirteen grandchildren was born in 1989, the last in 2009.

The hardest thing to write about is a happy marriage, and I have been blessed by one. Joanne and I married in Wayland, Massachusetts, a year after I met her and spilled grape juice on her dress at a children's party. She is a quite wonderful wife (patient and supportive) and a quite fabulous mother (accepting and caring). I often marvel at how she has stuck with me, since we are so different in so many ways. She likes to settle in one place. I have been open to moving about. She cherishes the past and I keep looking ahead (or did). She values close friendships. I have good friends, but none I would call really close. Joanne is interested in botany and her book clubs. I am interested in writing and in whatever jobs are on my desk at the moment. She reads a great deal. I read only a little.

What do we have in common? What binds us? Above all, our children and grandchildren (now, including their spouses, adding up to 27 people). They are an admirable bunch. What else? We loved dancing—folk, square, English country, and ballroom—and danced often. We enjoyed travel. We enjoyed and continue to enjoy many of the same arts performances. We think alike politically and share moral standards and principles of behavior. We recognize the importance of physical closeness.

Also, we have Shunk as a fixed point in our universe. Joanne grew up in the village of Shunk in northern Pennsylvania. Her far-seeing parents acquired a thousand-acre plot of forested land about five miles away from Shunk, and created a lake on it (large enough for swimming, sailing, canoeing, and kayaking). Now that land belongs to a corporate entity owned jointly by the extended families of Joanne and her brother, Dale. Each family has a house bordering the lake; ours has been occupied every summer since it was built in 1970.

Thank you, Joanne, for that heritage and for everything else you have done for me and for our children and their children over the years. I dedicate these essays to you, with love.

Ken Ford

EARLIEST MEMORIES

Two to seven

In my first year of life, I lived in three places: West Palm Beach, Florida, where I was born on May 1, 1926; Miami Beach, Florida, where I endured the famous Miami hurricane of September 1926 (in a dresser drawer, as later related by my mother); and in St. Matthews, Kentucky, a suburb of Louisville. My earliest memories are of St. Matthews, where I lived until I was seven.

The earliest thing I remember occurred when I was two, or perhaps not quite two. We lived in a first-floor apartment. I had evidently walked out the door into a hallway and crawled up a long straight flight of stairs to the second story, where I sat on the top step, perhaps preparatory to descending. I don't remember getting there. I only remember the cries of fear and anguish from my mother and one or two other women when they came into the hallway and saw me. I was rescued. No harm done, but a first memory implanted.

Around age three or four I was given set of blocks for Christmas or a birthday. I loved them the way some children love a doll or a teddy bear or a blanket. I made roads and buildings and towers with them and learned the alphabet with them. There were 27 cubical blocks in a box, arrayed in three rows of nine. The first block in the first row had pictures on its sides but no large letter. On each of the other 26 blocks there was a large letter on one face and pictures on the other faces. Every night I put the blocks back in their box in the exactly correct order with the letters showing on top. Today when I think of the alphabet I still see that box clearly: A through H in the first row, I through Q in the second row, R through Z in the third row, just as they should be.

Ken (2½) and Middy Ruth (6½), St. Matthews, Kentucky

There was no public kindergarten in St. Matthews. I was sent to a private kindergarten. I remember that it was on the second floor of a commercial building and that I was delivered and picked up every day by my mother. I must have been reading by that time, but the only thing I remember about kindergarten was the art—lots of paper, lots of crayons, lots of paint.

The next year, I walked by myself to first grade and was also allowed to visit the town library on my own and to check out books, which I continued to do in second grade (until, in the spring of my second-grade year, we moved to a different suburb, Buechel, with no easily accessible library). My first- and second-grade reading taste ran to the Wizard of Oz, Tom Sawyer, and the Hardy Boys.

Somewhere along about six or seven, my parents gave me a small black-and-white bulldog as a gift. I was asked to pick a name for her, and chose Giftie. Giftie and I didn't bond. I really didn't like Giftie and I was pretty sure she didn't like me. When we moved to Buechel my parents allowed me to give Giftie as a gift to a friend.

Of course my early memories include my mother (vividly); my father (pretty clearly); and my sister Middy Ruth (a bit more vaguely). MR (as we sometimes called her) was four years older than I and we led our own lives. Years later, as adults, we were very close. The arrival of younger sister Nancy in late August 1933, when I was seven, is memorable mainly because of my mother's distress in the final two months of her pregnancy. That summer was very hot and very humid (there was, of course, no air conditioning). Even as a little boy, I was pained to see my mother (then forty) sitting day after day in a porch swing fanning herself, trying to get comfortable, trying to get cool.

Not a lot of memories, but some interesting ones.

Nancy (6 mos.), Middy Ruth (7½), and Ken (11½), February 1934, Louisville, Kentucky

Middy Ruth, Ken, Nancy, and Giftie, 1937, Ft. Thomas, Kentucky

GEORGIA

A transplanted boy

When you are an eight-year-old white boy transplanted into the Jim Crow south, as I was in early 1935, you don't judge social conditions, you accept them. That's just the way the world is. Water fountains and rest rooms are labeled, "White" and "Colored." "Colored people" step off the sidewalk into the street if a white person approaches. The lone movie theater, or so I was told, had a balcony in which "colored people" could sit.

Middy Ruth (14), Ken (10), and Nancy (3), 1936, Ft. Thomas, Kentucky

I lived with my parents (both then 41) and my two sisters (Middy Ruth, 12, and one-year-old Nancy) on the first floor of a large house—sort of a modern plantation house—on a cotton-and-tobacco farm in rural Georgia, about midway between Reidsville and Collins, towns seven miles apart. Mrs. Breen, the farm's owner and manager, lived on the second floor. Why she needed to rent out part of her house is a question I didn't ask then and didn't think about later. The farm seemed to thrive. I saw the tobacco being harvested, cured, and sold. I saw the cotton being picked (I helped a little) and baled and sold. Sugar cane was grown, too, and watermelons. I don't know if they were sold.

Two black families worked for Mrs. Breen. Each family had a house—a shack, really—that contained numerous people—parents, children, and at least one grandparent. Those able to work did so. I have no idea how many rooms each house contained—or how many people. Each of these houses was fifty or so yards from the main house. Because I was young, I was allowed to visit those houses and to play with some of the black children (a privilege not afforded my older sister). Their houses sat on cinder-block supports. Oddly, what I especially remember about the houses is that looking down through gaps in the living-room flooring, you could see chickens and pigs wandering about underneath.

The property also contained a tobacco-curing barn and a few other outbuildings to house chickens, mules, wagons, and a few cows. My family rented one cow, assuring our supply of milk and butter. We didn't do the milking, but my mother made the butter by patiently shaking a two-quart Mason jar of cream until, miraculously, the butter appeared.

I'm pretty sure (now, in retrospect) that the black families were sharecroppers, not tenant farmers—since they didn't manage the farm. Mrs. Breen, the owner, was right there doing the daily managing. So the black families would have been assigned a share of the income from cotton and tobacco sales. They were also paid directly for some jobs such as housework and cotton picking. I remember the rate of pay for cotton picking—one cent per pound. I remember because I joined in the picking and earned 26 cents for a day's work. Strong young black men could earn more than a dollar a day. Girls and women pitched in, too. The cotton picker walks down rows between cotton plants dragging a large burlap bag behind. Each cotton boll needs to be handled just so as it is pulled from the plant and placed in the bag. It takes a lot of bolls to weigh a pound.

In the spring and in the fall of that year (when I was in the third and fourth grades), I rode on a bus to a brick schoolhouse in Collins. My black friends walked to a wooden schoolhouse outside of town (a fact that I just accepted as the way the world is). Despite its solid structure, my school lacked indoor plumbing. The outdoor toilet for boys was, as I recall, a "five-holer." Presumably the girls had a similar amenity. The school yard, like our yard back at Mrs. Breen's house, was sand, not grass. Our yard got raked, not mowed. (That was one of my chores.) The farm's chickens roamed about within a fenced area. They did not stray into the part of the yard where I had my elaborate

construction of roads and tunnels for my numerous toy cars. At school the yard was less well cared for. The chickens were not constrained, and all over the schoolyard they deposited what was called chicken dirt and which made it necessary to step carefully.

The chicken dirt had something to do with my least agreeable experience at the school. I was routinely mocked by my fellow students (just the boys, not the girls) for being "teacher's pet" and for my "Yankee accent" (acquired in Kentucky). One day, just after school let out, the hostility boiled over. I was held down in the school yard, and chicken dirt was smeared all over me. I was so distraught and smelled so bad that I couldn't bring myself to board the bus. I set off running for home. The bus, after discharging other children along the way, caught up with me, half running, half walking, when I was only a few hundred yards from home. The driver stopped the bus and offered me a ride, but I declined. I hadn't yet cried, but the moment I arrived at home, the tears flowed. My mother got me cleaned up. listened to my tale, and comforted me. That evening, the whole family discussed the incident and what to do about it. My parents decided not to report it. They advised me to go back to school and act as if it hadn't happened. That's what I did. My fellow students, too, acted as if it hadn't happened, and nothing like it happened again.

*   *   *   *   *

It's time to say why I was in Georgia. It had to do with the Depression and the country's slow climb out of it. In late 1933, when I was seven and when we lived in St. Matthews, a suburb of Louisville, my father lost his civil engineering job with a construction company. It was the first time—in fact, the only time—I saw my father cry. He came home, told my mother that he had been laid off, then threw himself on their bed and sobbed. Before long he found another job, as a factory worker on the graveyard shift (midnight to eight) at Brown and Williamson, a tobacco company (which became notorious decades later for blatantly putting profits ahead of public health). This required belt tightening in the family. The five of us (Nancy was a few months old and Middy Ruth was eleven) left our rented house in St. Matthews and moved to a smaller house in Buechel, a more distant suburb. I don't remember much about the Buechel house, which had apparently been someone's vacation home. I do remember that its kitchen stove used kerosene. Middy Ruth and I underwent a bit of hazing as we entered the second and sixth grades, but we adapted. I always liked school.

Middy Ruth (15), Ken (11), and Nancy (4) with grandparents Franklin and Cora Ford, 1937, Ft. Thomas, Kentucky

The Buechel experience must have lasted a little over a year, for me the latter part of second grade and the first part of third grade. My father was able to commute to his factory job in the family's 1932 Chevrolet, acquired before hard times hit. He was, of course, looking all the time for better work. His break came in early 1935, when he was offered a job as a civil engineer on a prison-building project in Reidsville, Georgia, funded by one of the recovery programs of the federal government. My mother, knowing it would be anything but easy for the family, nevertheless encouraged him to take it. He went first, and lived in a rented room in Reidsville while searching for family housing. The Breen farm turned out to be a happy choice for all of us.

I don't know how my father got to and from his Georgia work before we joined him. He had left the car with my mother. He was not able to return to Buechel to oversee or participate in the move, so it was up to my mother to load the car to its limit with belongings and children and head south. I remember only two things about that trip: that the floor space behind the car's front seat was Nancy's play area and bed and that we spent one night in a tourist cabin, a new and exciting experience for me.

Building a building, even a large prison, doesn't take a terribly long time. If you've been hired just to work on that building with nothing else assured, you will be looking for the next job from the day you start this one. My father's performance evidently pleased his Reidsville boss, not surprising considering my father's work ethic and his prior experience. As the prison job was wrapping up, he was offered a job with better pay and more responsibility in one of the New Deal's "alphabet" agencies—the Public Works Administration (PWA). The job was to travel around Kentucky, inspecting and overseeing work on numerous PWA projects—mainly schools and courthouses. Why my parents chose Ft. Thomas, a Cincinnati suburb in northern Kentucky, rather than the Louisville area as the place to live I don't know. But that was their choice. Once more, Middy Ruth and I were uprooted from school (I didn't really mind) and transported somewhere else. So I landed in Ft. Thomas at age nine for the latter part of the fourth grade, and stayed there until I was sixteen. In the fall of 1942 I boarded a train in Cincinnati (my first train ride ever) and headed for my junior year at Exeter (where it was—and still is—called the upper middle year).

*   *   *   *   *

Back to Georgia: Outside of school, I was mostly alone, reading or organizing my toy-car village in the yard. My father did take me on some outings, and with him I got to see my first water moccasins and coral snakes. Snakes, harmless and otherwise, were plentiful in Georgia. An acquaintance with a pickup truck brought a dead diamondback rattler to be viewed, laid out straight in our yard. One day, Middy Ruth's scream brought me to the chicken house where I got a look at a very imposing although harmless chicken snake, as long as a man is tall, lolling in the rafters. One of the black workers disposed of it.

Spreading adders were common in the dusty washboard road that ran by our house. These roads—hard baked in dry weather, slippery in wet weather, and bone-jarringly rough on cars driven fast in any weather—were well named. Most housewives in that place and at the time (although not my mother) did their laundry by rubbing wet and soapy clothes on the knurled ridges of washboards. For mules pulling wagons and for boys in bare feet, though, these roads were just fine. I liked the feel of them, and didn't mind stepping on the occasional adder, easy to do since their color matched the road color.

Water moccasins were reputedly present in the Ohoopee River, where I learned to swim, but I never saw one there. Middy Ruth was my swimming instructor. She told me to walk down the very steep bank into the water, keep going until the water was up to my chin or beyond, then turn around and paddle back to shore. Frightening but effective pedagogy. I learned to love swimming but always in my own amateurish way. (So it went later with other sports—tennis, squash, skiing—never a professional lesson in any of them.)

I especially enjoyed Saturday visits to the prison work site, where I could walk on half-built concrete walls and sight through a surveyor's transit. Also on Saturdays, with a little help from my father, I earned some money selling magazines in Reidsville (see "Gainful Employment").

I had no close friends at or near my age in Georgia. I walked sometimes to the next farm to the north, where I spent some time with a white boy from school. I now remember more about how his family did their laundry than I remember our interaction. They had two large washbasins perched on a board held up by sawhorses, one basin full of warm, soapy wash water, the other full of cold rinse water. The only wringers were human hands. I remember the adults' powerful hands. As mentioned, I played sometimes with black children on Mrs. Breen's farm, but made no real friendships among them. Perhaps they were too deferential, perhaps I was unwilling to fully share my toy car universe.

But I did have one good friend, Uncle Billy. He was the patriarch of one of the black families, a father and a grandfather, perhaps in his seventies, perhaps still in his sixties. He still worked hard, and directed the younger workers. Uncle Billy took me under his wing. He taught me how to drive a mule ("haw" means left and "gee" means right) and how to suck sweet goodness from a sugar cane stalk. He showed me how tobacco leaves were tied to long sticks called laths and dried in a curing barn, and he taught me how to pick cotton.

When the cotton had all been picked, it was loaded into a wagon with high sides, pulled by two mules. Uncle Billy sat up front holding the reins and invited me to join him. As we rolled slowly toward the cotton gin in Collins, we talked, and he let me handle the reins. I watched the cotton being vacuumed into the gin, and watched as the now-seedless cotton was compressed into bales and the bales were bound by steel straps and loaded back in the wagon. By now it was late afternoon and we headed back to the farm. I took the reins. I was on top of the wagon and on top of the world.

*   *   *   *   *

In December 2002, on my way to Florida by car, I stopped in Collins. The two-story brick schoolhouse with its wooden outdoor toilets was gone, replaced by a generic one-story structure that looked like any other grade school in any other place, and surely had indoor toilets. The town, with a reported population of 528 at that time, was no bigger than it was sixty-seven years earlier, but with some grass where there had been sand. I drove down the now-paved road toward Reidsville, and there it was—Mrs. Breen's farmhouse, where I had been the wide-eyed observer of a different culture. The tobacco-curing barn was still standing, although in serious disrepair. I could see no remnant at all of the two shanties where the multi-generational black sharecropper families had lived. Their houses, like the culture of which they were a part, had vanished totally. Because of the season, I couldn't tell what was now being grown in the surrounding fields. And, of course, I had no idea who was now cultivating the fields.

LITTLE ORPHAN ANNIE

Early teens

"Quiz Kids" was a radio show launched in 1940 in which precocious children under the age of 16 were asked questions and given small prizes for correct answers. It was modeled after the already very popular show "Information Please," in which adults competed for prizes. Several kids, with particularly astonishing funds of knowledge, were regulars. Others came and went.

1944 Advertisement for Quiz Kids radio show

The show originated in Chicago. From time to time it was broadcast from other cities, with guest participants recruited from those cities. When it was due to air in Cincinnati, in late 1940 or early 1941 (when I was 14 and a ninth-grader), the call went out for local recruits (my town of Ft. Thomas, Kentucky, just across the Ohio River, was considered "local"). I don't remember how I got to be among the final half dozen or so who were finalists to become the one local teen to appear on the show when it came to town. We assembled in a room in the city and were quizzed. As I recall, it was run like a spelling bee—that is, you were eliminated if you got one answer wrong. I was hanging in there with correct answers on science, geography, and history. Then I was asked, "What is the color of Little Orphan Annie's hair." I didn't know. I guessed, and I guessed wrong. I was out.

I was angry—not at myself, but at the organizers of the quiz. Who *cares,* I asked myself, what color Little Orphan Annie's hair is? Why should it matter whether I know or don't know? It wasn't fair, I told myself, to have my intellect judged on the basis of my familiarity with something in popular culture. As it happened, I *did* read the Little Orphan Annie comic strip, but in its daily black-and-white version, not in its Sunday colored version. So I didn't know that she had red hair. (As I thought about it later, I decided that it was, after all, a reasonable question, and that I should have been able to figure out the answer. Red headed girls were supposedly more feisty, more independent than blonds and brunettes. Being a reader of the strip, I knew Little Orphan Annie's character, and I should have reasoned that her creators would give this supercharged girl red hair to fit a stereotype.)

I did not have a "helicopter parent." I was never pushed, never tutored, never praised in any but muted tones. And I never consciously pushed myself. As a child and teen-ager, I did all the same things that my young companions did. I fashioned sand highways and sand cities for my collection of little metal cars. I rode my red wagon when that was all that Santa could afford to give me, and later my bicycle when the family economy improved. I climbed trees and played hide-and-seek. I bought penny candy and I read and collected and traded comic books. If I differed a little from my companions, it was in how many books I read. I wasn't pushed to do so, and it wasn't because I thought I "should" read a lot. I was just interested. It was an agreeable way to spend my time. Beginning in first grade, I took books from the local library, including all the Oz books and many books about the crime-fighting exploits of teens. In the ninth and tenth grades, my interests turned scientific, and I read just about every book of science and scientific biography that was in the Fort Thomas high school library. (I recall one on Galileo that led me to attach a small light to the rim of the wheel on a toy wind-up tractor, and use my parents' Brownie camera to take a time-exposure of the tractor rolling across my bedroom floor in order to get an image of a cycloid, a curve probably discovered well before Galileo but attributed to him in the biography I read.)

Ken at Phillips Exeter Academy, Spring 1944

So what was going on? Why was I chosen to compete in the Quiz Kids competition? Why did some teachers both in Georgia and Kentucky ask me to sit in the back of the class and work at my own pace? Why was I singled out to be recommended for a "regional scholarship" to Exeter, and why was it awarded? Why did I go to Washington as a Science Talent Search winner and why did I finish first in my class at Exeter? Why was I admitted without fuss or fanfare (and without the least angst) to Harvard and Princeton? Why did I graduate *summa cum laude* from Harvard? Why, in Navy electronic technician training, did I finish first or second in my class of a hundred or so when class rankings were posted every week? I honestly don't know. It's true that I liked to please my teachers, and it's also true that I hated to fail, as in the Quiz Kids competition. But coming out on the top of the heap was never my intention. It was not to please my parents. It was not to prove anything, or to upstage my fellow students. It was not to gain adulation. It just happened. Which means, I suppose, that DNA is the answer.

Eventually, of course, one finds oneself below the top in the peer groups one joins. As an adult, I succeeded, perhaps scored even a bit above average, in three peer groups: theoretical physicists, teachers, and writers. I am happy to have been part of each of these groups. Never have I had the least sense of failure in not being a superstar in any of them.

There is one peer group in which my accomplishment has been below average—a mid-career Little

Edith and Ken at his Harvard graduation, 1948

Orphan Annie. That is the group of college presidents. Some people have a natural talent for management, be it educational or other. Some can acquire the talent by study and practice. Some, like me, think it can't be very hard and dive in without the natural talent and without studying. We stub our toes and think how it might have been but wasn't. (See "On Being a College President.")

Edith, Ken, and Paul at his Harvard graduation, 1948

REBELLION

Late teens

I think of myself as a person of moral rectitude. I don't steal or cheat, and I try not to lie. If I were to find a money-filled wallet on the street, I would make every effort to return it intact to its owner. But there is something about arbitrary authority that brings out the rebel in me. (See "Oaths, Signed and Unsigned.") Here's an early example: At age 12 or thereabouts, I refused to go to Boy Scout camp despite urging by my parents. I feared that at camp, I would lose the freedoms I then enjoyed—to climb a tree, ride a bike, or read a book whenever I wanted to. I assumed that in camp I would be told what to do, and when. I didn't like the idea.

Ken in the Navy

At age 19 in the Navy, I lined up for inspection wearing white socks on a day we were required to wear our blue uniforms and dark socks. The inspecting Chief Petty Officer noticed and asked me why I was wearing white socks. "I have a chit," I answered. At the time, we carried a small pad of "chits." For each infraction called out by a superior, we handed over a chit, on which the officer wrote the time, date, place, and nature of the infraction. The chits were collected and their contents dutifully recorded somewhere. On this occasion, the CPO, assuming that no sane sailor would wear white socks without a good reason, assumed that my chit was a doctor's permission to wear white socks (perhaps because of athlete's foot). He grumbled something to that effect and moved on.

What was it about the Navy? Little acts of rebellion continued. Later the same year I was an Apprentice Seaman (and a sophomore) in the Navy's V-12 program at the University of Michigan in Ann Arbor. It was 1945. I was 19. The Navy's rules were hardly onerous. Except for one required Navy course (it was called "Damage Control" and dealt with keeping ships afloat after they had been damaged by mines or torpedoes), I had full freedom to select my courses. And except for a requirement that I be in the dorm by 9:00 p.m., I was free to spend my time as I saw fit. Well, not completely free. One afternoon a week, we sailors were to line up on a playing field for marching drill and exercises. I handled that requirement by finding and enrolling in a physics course whose lab met that afternoon, thus gaining me exemption from the drill. I handled the required Navy course differently. I decided to give it three hours a week. I attended the class meetings, doing all of my reading and homework in class, but, as a matter of principle, paying no attention to the course between its class meetings. For this hubris I paid a price. At the end of the semester, I received a B in Damage Control while earning A's in all my other courses.

Middy Ruth, Nancy, Edith, Ken

Yet, for reasons I don't pretend to understand, I had to rebel, and was willing to push the limits to do so. In the spring of 1946, just before and just after my twentieth birthday (May 1), still in Ann Arbor and with the end of my Navy service approaching, I worked several nights a week as a waiter in an on-campus restaurant. There are things about this escapade (it deserves to be called that) that I don't remember. How I learned about the job. How I applied for it. Who interviewed me. How I got paid. How I transferred a set of civilian clothes from my parents' home in Cleveland to the back of a closet in my Ann Arbor dorm (where, when I was not working, Navy uniforms in front of them hid them from the view of our not-too-meticulous inspectors). Also not remembered: what hours I worked (possibly 9:00 to 11:00 p.m.), how many days a week I worked (probably about three), and how many weeks I worked (probably five or six).

But there are some things I remember clearly.

A fellow sailor introduced me to a large, dry, well-lighted utility tunnel with unlocked doors that afforded a path from the basement of my dorm to another building not far away. From there I could stroll across campus to my workplace. Mostly I waited tables. My co-workers, alert and helpful, kept an eye out for Navy officers. If one came into the restaurant, I was given an immediate high sign. I then ducked into the kitchen to assist with food preparation and dishwashing until the officer, who might have recognized me, departed.

My boss was a young woman, probably no more than five years older than I. I'll call her Marjorie. Sometimes, after the restaurant closed and was cleaned up, I walked with her to her nearby apartment. We seemed to have a lot to talk about, on the walks and afterwards in her apartment. We both had our dreams—mine to become a physicist and hers to manage a first-class hotel. In her apartment, we might talk for a long time as I brushed her long dark hair. After we parted, with a kiss, I would make my way back across campus, walk through the utility tunnel, carefully hang up my civilian clothes, and get some sleep.

Sometimes the sleeping was done in her bed, not mine. But we were kissing cousins, not lovers. It was a special relationship for both of us, all the sweeter for its restraint. When I slept with Marjorie, I would be up and off by 7:00 in order to avoid accidental contact with a Navy officer on my way back to my dorm. If it was a Saturday or Sunday morning, I might skip breakfast and catch a bit more sleep in my bunk.

Marjorie and I never communicated after that spring. We both sensed that our little romance was ephemeral and that it was special, better kept locked in our memories than kept alive through some inevitably sterile means—letters or phone calls. So I never learned if Marjorie got her hotel nor whether she married and had children.

I skated on thin ice. Miraculously, I wasn't found out. I broke no state or federal laws. I didn't harm the Navy. It's 75 years later and I have no regrets.

Ken and his touring bicycle (Boston to Cleveland and back to New York), summer 1948

MOTHER

The remarkable Mrs. Ford

My mother, Edith Timblin, was born in 1892 and died in 1992. She left this world three days before her one-hundredth birthday. She wanted to reach that birthday so that she would appear on the *Today* show. It's just as well that her iron will failed her this time, for she would have been disappointed. She didn't know that NBC, in the face of ever more centenarians, had raised the bar for an appearance to 103 or 104.

Why did she want to be on the *Today* show? Because, all her life, she wanted to rise above her beginnings, to be somebody, to be seen as remarkable. That's how I described her when I spoke at her memorial service in the Presbyterian Church of Shelby, North Carolina—the remarkable Mrs. Ford. That's what her friends called her. That's how we, her grown-up children, thought of her. I never heard her called sweet. No one thought of her as soft. She was "intelligent," sometimes "amazing," always "remarkable." Did I detect in the minister's eulogy just a hint of relief? No longer would he have to cope with her questions, her doubts about the literal truth of the Bible, her challenges to his beliefs.

My mother's life was defined by two things she didn't do. She didn't grow up in a middle-class family with linen and crystal and china, and she didn't go to college.

When my mother was about twelve, her mother died. Her father was not much of a provider and not much of a father. Mother spoke little of him, just enough to make us children imagine that he was a very bad man indeed. Only once were we allowed to meet this grandfather, and then just briefly. His sins, we were later made to understand, included drinking and carrying on with women.

I never learned whether my mother felt any sympathy for her father, any understanding of his waywardness, any love for him. I suspect that what she wanted was to feel nothing—no love, no hatred—only to build a wall. Entering her teen years without a mother and with a father who provided little money and, in her eyes, behaved abhorrently, she had to mature quickly.

As soon as my mother finished high school, which included business courses, she went to work. She started as a secretary, became a Comptometer operator, then a Comptometer instructor. (A Comptometer was a mechanical device with a crank and gears, the predecessor of a desk calculator.) Edith was the second of four girls. Her older sister, Geneva, had no inclination for college. She married young. Mother's two younger sisters, Elizabeth and Mildred, were more intellectually inclined, and my mother helped pay for their college costs. Elizabeth became a teacher. Mildred became the wife of a CPA.

Mother read more, thought more, argued more, wrote more, traveled more, and took more adult courses than the great majority of her college-graduate friends. She cared about learning and she cared about status. In her eighties, she took correspondence courses and wrote book reviews for the local paper. When she was past ninety, she took second prize in a beauty and talent contest for seniors. (We liked to remind her that it was as if she had drawn a Community Chest card in Monopoly.)

I was Mother's only son. She had two daughters, one four years older than I, the other seven years younger than I. All of us were expected, as a matter of course, to go to college. It's very hard for me to say whether high achievement was "expected" of me. I knew only that high achievement was treated as the norm. If I came home with an all-A report card, Mother might say "That's nice" in a tone

Ken and Edith, Shelby, North Carolina, 1962

Edith, Socorro, New Mexico, 1977

suggesting that anything else would have been a surprise. She was quick to comment on my posture or my manners but not on my school work. I think she decided early that she had an unusually talented son on her hands. Since she couldn't do much one way or the other about my intellect, she would work on my behavior—and on my matrimonial prospects. When I went out with an Italian-American girl who was Catholic, Mother's disapproval was palpable. When I became friends with a Wellesley girl who was Presbyterian and whose father was a wealthy bond trader in New York, Mother effusively praised my sound judgment.

My mother and father were 26 when they met in church, 27 when they got married. My father Paul was a civil engineer who touched no alcohol and had the total decency that my mother needed. He read *Field and Stream* or *Outdoor Life* while she read Tolstoy or Dickens. She went along uncomplainingly to read in the car or on a spread-out blanket while he fished. He learned to play bridge and Scrabble, and was a good host at the dinners my mother arranged. They made friends and kept them.

My mother handled the family finances. When the family moved, which, because of my father's work, was often, my mother was the chief of logistics. She made arrangements with the moving van company, dealt with landlords, the gas company, the electric company, and the post office, and personally packed the car so that every cubic inch of its trunk was efficiently used.

My mother lived as a widow for 32 years after my father's death of a stroke at 68. In practical terms, the transition was not so difficult, since she had always been in charge. Whatever her grief, it was private. To show her emotion would have been to show weakness. She remained the remarkable Mrs. Ford, active in church and community, keeping her mind in gear, keeping up a large correspondence.

I wrote to my mother often as a young man, and even as an adult. When we were together, we played games, discussed issues of the day, and joked. Maybe I had to joke. Even she could see the humor in her persistent efforts to set me straight on matters of politics, morals, and matrimony.

During the depression, after doing manual labor for a time, my father gained a job in his profession with a U.S. government agency, the Public Works Administration. He therefore felt it necessary, in 1936, to vote Democratic, something he had never done before. He cast his vote for Franklin Roosevelt. By 1940 he was back in the Republican fold. Years later, after his death, my mother told me privately that she had not weakened in 1936. Although she never told her husband, she voted for Alf Landon that year. Principles are principles.

And her only son is a liberal Democrat. Who didn't marry the Wellesley girl.

Karin and Ken's father Paul, 1952

SEX

Brief remarks on an infinitely interesting subject

When I was a young physics professor at Brandeis University, a female undergraduate asked me, "Do you think that sex before marriage is OK?" (This was at a party at another professor's house, not in my office. And it was at a time when such questions occurred to people.) I answered, "Well, I am not opposed to the idea in principle. But it is such a powerful emotional experience, more so than almost anything else you might do, that I don't think it's something that should be undertaken lightly."

When I was a not-so-young physics professor at U Mass Boston, some of my students were above typical college age, being the first in their families to go to college. Sometimes I would join one or more of these older students for conversation in the campus coffee shop. I was interested to learn about their backgrounds. At one such meeting, a female student who had raced cars professionally said to me, "You have just made physics come alive for me. Sometimes, when I am reading *Scientific American*, I get so excited that I have an orgasm." "Well," I said, "That's interesting."

Sex in marriage, I have learned, is important. For many decades.

That's all I have to say on the subject.

BITTE

A young man in Germany

How I ended up in bed with Anneliese is not a long story. When you are 23 and have had a bit of wine and the young lady knows what she wants, it can happen.

It was the summer of 1949, the first time after the Second World War that foreign tourists were allowed into Germany. I had finished my first year of graduate school and decided to explore Europe. A friend and I flew to Shannon, Ireland, bought bicycles, and set out. After a month or so of youth hostels and highways and byways, we separated by prearrangement in Holland. He pedaled off into France, and I into Germany.

I had signed up for a two-week international student symposium that began and ended in Göttingen, an ancient university town famous for its past glories in science and mathematics. It had suffered little war damage and was now occupied by the British. The symposium was to be a road show so that we could see cities that had been totally leveled as well as some that had been untouched, and could see, too, the vigorous rebuilding effort then getting under way.

We young people from various nations were to get together in a war-ravaged country to discuss peace and friendship, to talk about a better future world. I was, as it turned out, the only American in the group. Among our German hosts—as among other young educated Germans at the time— there was a sense of abandon, of living for the moment. We aliens came with serious purpose. Our hosts, only then recovering from hunger and privation, wanted to party more than ponder, to dance more than discuss.

Anneliese, 19, was the symposium secretary. She made travel and hotel arrangements and helped generally with logistics. Before our arrival, she had lined up willing families in Göttingen and assigned participants to bunk with them. Perhaps because I was the lone American, she assigned me to the couch in the combined living room-dining room of the apartment where she lived with her mother.

On my very first night there, she sat and talked and snuggled until her mother, calling from another room, ordered her to her own room. Anneliese's evening warmth grew over the next couple of days. I was quite taken with this beautiful, fresh-faced German girl. I decided that Anneliese's name was about the loveliest I had ever heard, and that she was as charming a girl as I had ever met.

Then it was on to Bochum and Braunschweig and Wolfsburg. In Bochum we went deep underground into a coal mine, then washed off the coal dust in segregated hot tubs while sipping cognac (all part of the tradition, we were assured). In the evening, wine flowed like water at a huge reception hosted by the Bochum city fathers. Anneliese and I hung out together like a high-school pair going steady. Later, In Wolfsburg, we would see a Volkswagen assembly line carrying suspended car parts from one building to another across a bombed-out field. But it's time to talk about Braunschweig.

After dining and dancing and singing and imbibing on our first evening in Braunschweig, I returned to the hotel with Anneliese. It seemed so natural that she should invite me into her room. And so natural that we were suddenly naked and in bed. We touched each other with growing passion. Anneliese rolled onto her back and said, "Bitte."

Suddenly, from somewhere deep within me, I was hearing another voice. It was saying, "Ken, why are you here? What's going on? What are you doing?" I hardly had time to think, but I grasped for time. To gain a few moments, I pretended not to know what Anneliese was asking. Her "Bitte" meant "Please." In other contexts, it can mean "You're welcome" or "I didn't quite understand. Please repeat."

"Bitte?" I asked. "Was heisst das?" (Bitte? What does it mean?)

"Du weisst shon," replied Anneliese. *"Bitte."* (You know perfectly well what it means. *Please.)*

The voice within me gained strength. Somehow, it miraculously trumped emotion. I paused a moment, and said quietly, "Ich kann nicht." (I can't.)

Anneliese rolled away from me without a word. I rolled against her back. We were both exhausted. We fell asleep.

I rose early, dressed, and went back to my room. At breakfast, Anneliese neither favored nor avoided me. She bestowed her pink-cheeked charm on all who were present. By that afternoon, she had a young Frenchman in her sights. For the next week they were inseparable.

In the evenings that followed, I pulled out the copy of A. E. Housman's *A Shropshire Lad* that I had toted across Europe on my bicycle and reflected on the pain of existence.

Oh, Dear Anneliese! That was many decades ago. You were so sweet. Can you imagine how many times I have thought of you, how many times I have wondered what became of you? How can you know that a little thrill runs through me whenever I chance to meet someone named Anneliese? I have had time aplenty to wonder why I said *no* to you.

On the road from Silverton to Ouray, Colorado, 1951

Utah desert, 1951

Madison, Wisconsin, 1951

New York City Harbor, taken from a ferry, 1951

Garden City, Long Island, New York, Christmas 1951

Dave Nason and his MG en route to Stowe, 1951

Ken, Nassau, Bahamas, 1952

Ken Standing, in Ken's Singer at Lake Carnegie, Princeton, New Jersey, 1952

KARIN

Joy and Remorse

I met Karin in the fall of 1948, at a Tuesday-night
folk dance in Princeton, New Jersey. She was 14.
I was 22. Karin had just arrived in America from
Germany. She was living on a farm across the Del-
aware River in Bucks County, Pennsylvania, and
was enrolled as a high-school freshman in the local public school in Doylestown. I had just arrived
in Princeton from Harvard and was beginning my
graduate work in physics at the University.

Karin Stehnike, Bucks County, Pennsylvania, 1952

Five years later, when Karin was 19 and I was 27, we were married in Los Alamos, New Mexico.

I remember that first meeting. Karin had pink cheeks and long blond braids; she was wearing a
dirndl. If I had pink cheeks, it was only because I blushed easily in the presence of attractive girls
and young women. I was wearing a button-down shirt with no tie, and sneakers. Although Karin,
at the time, had been in America for at most a few weeks, she already spoke acceptable English.
(Four years later, she won a prize as the top English student in her graduating class.) My German
was shaky, but I wanted to practice it. For that reason, and to be hospitable to a new dancer, I
chatted with Karin.

I had been introduced to folk dancing four years earlier, in Woods Hole, Massachusetts, where,
following my graduation from Phillips Exeter Academy in New Hampshire, I spent the summer
of 1944 as a stockroom assistant at the Marine Biological Lab while awaiting a call from the U.
S. Navy—a call that came in September. Why Woods Hole? Because my Exeter physics teacher,
Bert Little, had a home and a summer job there, and invited me to join him. Why folk dancing?
Because Bert Little's wife, Barbara, was an enthusiastic dancer who rounded up all within reach
to share in her enthusiasms. I enjoyed dancing but didn't follow up until I got to Princeton. And
then it wasn't a love of dancing that led me to the Tuesday-night folk dances so much as it was the
desire to meet girls (as we then called every female person under 30). Princeton's undergraduates
were then all male, and its graduate students were overwhelmingly so. The folk dances, however,
drew many young women from the town of Princeton and from surrounding towns as far afield as
Trenton and New Hope and Doylestown.

Among the regulars were several high-school girls from Bucks County, including Louise Ganter and Anneke van Kirk (at least one of whom was of driving age). It was Louise's parents who took in Karin at their Mechanicsville farm, so it was natural that Karin would be invited to join the small going-to-Princeton gang on Tuesday evenings. (It's hardly relevant to my story, but I can't help mentioning that Rainer Weiss, who won the 2017 Nobel Prize in physics, was, in his youth, enamored of Louise; and that Anneke later married Woody Guthrie, an event that enabled Karin and me to meet Woody and to hear him sing, over and over, "Good Night, Irene.")

Karin had been born in New York in 1934, the first of her parents' five children and the only one born in America. Her parents, Kurt and Elise Stehnike, both immigrants from Germany, had met and married in New York. For whatever reason—perhaps they were struggling to make ends meet, perhaps they were homesick, perhaps they were drawn to the possibilities in Hitler's new Germany, perhaps all three—they returned to Germany when Karin was a baby. By her recollection, her childhood there was happy. Her father served in the Army; four more children were added to the family; aunts and uncles and cousins were nearby.

In the spring of 1945, when the war in Europe approached its end, the Stehnike's road became rocky. For safety, the family moved to Schleswig-Holstein, the region of Germany closest to Denmark, where Elise had grown up. Kurt went AWOL—either to shepherd his family to their new home or to visit them there. In April 1945, less than a month before the war in Europe ended, he was apprehended, arrested, given a summary trial, and shot. I later visited the cemetery where he is buried. Adjacent to the simple stone marker over his grave are an array of others, each labeled with a soldier's name and an April 1945 date.

* * * * *

Karin and Ken, Lake Peak, New Mexico, 1953

Karin and I continued to enjoy dancing and talking on Tuesday nights. In 1950, when I was 24, I "disappeared" for a year to Los Alamos. When I returned, our friendship resumed in a very natural way. In the summer of 1951, three years after she had arrived, when she was 17 and I was 25, I asked her out on a date—to attend a summer theater performance, if I remember correctly. Then, for another two years, she was, if not my "girlfriend," at least a special friend. We went out together to plays and concerts, including once to hear the Philadelphia Orchestra, then conducted by Eugene Ormandy. We danced the hambo and a lot of other favorites. We sat in diners talking for as much as an hour at a time. We seemed to think alike on a lot of topics, and found the same things funny. Ours was what in those days was called a "Platonic" relationship, but a relationship it was.

In 1952, at age 18, Karin graduated from high school with honors and took an office job in Trenton (just ten miles from Princeton). Neither the Ganters nor Karin's mother (who, by this time, was living on a small farm in Florida with her other four children and a new husband) suggested college. I must have done so, for the next spring (a year after high-school graduation) she applied to Barnard College in New York and was admitted. I don't know where the money for college was to come from. Her mother had no money and the Ganters were unlikely to supply any. Perhaps she planned to save from her Trenton earnings and continue part-time work in New York. She and I must have talked about it. I just don't remember. In any case, she was able to afford a small apartment in Trenton. We continued to see each other, at dances and on "dates."

After wrapping up my work in the H-bomb project in the fall of 1952, I pitched into my dissertation research and, within six months, was ready to start writing (with a fountain pen) what turned out to be a 219-page tome called "Applications of the Collective Model of the Nucleus." I turned to my best friend, who, by this time was an excellent typist, to see if she could type the dissertation onto master sheets for duplication and then handle the duplication. She could, and she did. (I paid her.) This meant that, for a month or so in the spring, we spent a lot of time together, evenings and weekends. I remember noticing at the time that Karin kept a copy of *War and Peace* always with her, and opened it to read a few pages whenever she took a break from working for me.

By May or June 1953, the dissertation was typed, duplicated, and distributed; I had successfully "defended" it and delivered a colloquium talk on its findings to Princeton's physics faculty and graduate students; and I was Dr. Ford.

I had accepted a job as a research associate at Indiana University, to start in September, and I planned to spend the summer at Los Alamos doing unclassified research. (By this time, I had such a good relationship with Los Alamos Lab's T Division that getting a summer job there was mostly a matter of notifying them that I was coming.) Karin and I did not talk about the future, for neither of us imagined that we had a "future." We just assumed that we would part company and go our separate ways, remembering a very special friendship.

For me, this perspective lasted at most a few weeks after I got to Los Alamos. Something important was missing from my life. I had no idea how important Karin had become until suddenly she wasn't there. At once it seemed the most natural thing in the world that I should propose marriage. On a return trip to Princeton in July, that's just what I did, and the proposal was accepted (meaning the Barnard plan was shelved). About a month later, Karin came to Los Alamos and stayed with John and Janette Wheeler, who were also there for the summer. Janette saw what I saw in Karin and approved of the union, even though she and Karin could hardly have had more different backgrounds. (By contrast, when I was briefly engaged two years earlier to a Los Alamos girl who was both very pretty and a very good dancer, Janette had said to me, through tears, "Take her to bed if you want to, Ken, but *don't* marry her.")

We were married in late August. Neither Karin's family nor mine attended, but quite a few Los Alamos scientists and staff were there. The guests included, as I recall, Enrico and Laura Fermi, Stan and Francoise Ulam, Edward and Mici Teller, Carson and Kay Mark, and Norris Bradbury (Carson was head of T Division, and Norris was head of the lab). One notable scientist who was not there was Hans Bethe. He responded to the Wheelers' invitation by saying "I don't do weddings."

Just as in the movies of the times, our first physical intimacy was on our wedding night. That was in a Best Western motel in Salida, Colorado. (Best Western was, at the time, a very small chain and was indeed western. I still feel warmly toward it.) Then we spent a few days in Aspen, and finished

Karin with John and Janette Wheeler, Leiden, Netherlands, 1956

off a week-long honeymoon by driving to sites of natural beauty in Colorado and Utah. Thanks to guidance and a referral by Janette Wheeler, we were able to postpone parenthood until we were ready, which was four years later.

Although our marriage lasted only seven years, I have almost exclusively agreeable memories of it. In Bloomington, Indiana, we danced (of course), including performing in a square-dance group in a farm show on a local TV station. I taught and did research, and flew my little Ercoupe. Karin enrolled as an IU student, selecting German literature as a major. I learned to play the recorder, and learned to love the madrigals that Karin and some of her friends sang.

In Göttingen, Germany, where we spent a year, I tried to broaden my research interests, under Werner Heisenberg's guidance, and my German slowly improved. Karin took a couple of "correspondence courses" from Indiana University, and audited a Göttingen course. We made friends and I drank Brüderschaft with Gerhart Lüders. (He was a colleague at the physics institute. He and his wife Inge lived in the same apartment complex as did Karin and I.)

In a couple of subsequent summers we separated for a month or so as Karin stayed in Bloomington to study and I went off to California to augment my University salary by consulting for aerospace companies (who hired the likes of me to help fulfill government contracts). We also spent a full year, 1957-58, at Los Alamos—a very good year. Paul was born there soon after our arrival, and he was a delightful one-year-old when we relocated to Waltham, MA at the end of that Los Alamos stay. If there were signs of trouble in our marriage, I was too obtuse to notice them.

Karin was pregnant when we arrived in Waltham in the late summer of 1958, and Sarah was born there in early December. I was caught up in my duties at Brandeis University, and Karin was caught up in child care. I helped occasionally with diaper changing and diaper washing (no diaper service then), also with reading to the children and taking them on walks, but mostly there was a clear division of duties—I at the university, Karin at home. At the same time, there was no shortage of parties and card games with fellow faculty, most of whom were also young. I joined a flying club at nearby Hanscom Field. Sadly, I can't remember now whether Karin took a course at Brandeis, and (also sadly), I can't remember to what extent I encouraged her continued university education. Certainly I recognized her intellect and academic potential, but I guess I didn't push her. Strange, in retrospect.

Karin and Paul (~2 weeks old),
Los Alamos, New Mexico, 1957

Beneath the superficial calm at home was Karin's growing anger. Beginning in the fall of 1959, she now and then unleashed her frustrations by shouting at me, often over something seemingly minor, and often in the presence of the children. She had a point. I was selfish. My work came first. And I wasn't astute enough to try to solve the problem or to propose counseling. Instead I walked away from the clamor—at first just to my office or the airport; finally, in the early summer of 1960, to the divorce court. My rationale at the time, which I now know to be almost surely wrong, was that the children would be better off in a stress-free single-parent home than in a high-decibel, high-stress two-parent home.

It worked out all right for me (if you overlook the scars). I paid as much attention as I could to Paul and Sarah. I remarried and now have seven children—Paul and Sarah and five others. Paul and Sarah spent most summers with the new family. We worked at making it one family, and, I think (I hope) largely succeeded.

It did not work out so well for Karin. Although she returned to Bloomington, earned a bachelor's degree, was elected to Phi Beta Kappa, and secured a responsible on-campus job, she did not re-marry and was, for the most part, not happy. She drank a little, then a lot. She died in 2008 at the age of 73.

The miracle in all this is that Paul and Sarah have emerged as extraordinary adults—bright, well balanced, happily married (once each), with remarkable children of their own. They both excelled in first-rate boarding schools, attended Ivy-League universities, and earned graduate degrees.

So the end of the marriage to Karin is something I live with, and something I think about every day. But I don't brood about it. There would be no point in that. When one makes a mistake—as I did—one can only try to compensate in whatever ways are possible, and now and then ponder the "what ifs."

Karin, Sarah, and Ken,
Wallingford, Connecticut, 1977

Joan's Job
A brush with fame

In August of 1958, Karin and I and our thirteen-month-old son, Paul, arrived in Waltham, Massachusetts, where I was to take up my new job as an associate professor of physics at Brandeis University. I was thirty-two; Karin was twenty-four and pregnant (our daughter, Sarah, arrived in December). We had, until then, lived only in furnished housing and were not yet weighed down by material things. The three of us and all our earthly possessions fit comfortably in the Ford coupe that had brought us from New Mexico in five days.

Joan Baez, 1965

Once we'd moved into our new home and had purchased some furniture and kitchen items, we decided that in the new location and with a growing family we needed another vehicle. Or at least *I* needed another vehicle. I learned that a gas station near Harvard Square sold Vespa motor scooters and also offered free riding lessons to first-time buyers. I called, ordered a gray Vespa with a windshield, and, in a few days, showed up in Cambridge to claim it.

I was introduced to my instructor. She was young, slender, and pretty, with long black hair. "Get on behind me," she said. "We'll ride across the river to the Soldier's Field parking lot and you can practice there." So I hung on, with her hair blowing in my face, as she deftly (someone watching might have said defiantly) maneuvered through traffic and across the Boyleston Street Bridge.

Once I had figured out how to start, steer, shift, and stop the Vespa in the parking lot, there was time for small talk. I introduced myself and asked her name. "Joan Baez," she said.

"Ah," I responded. "An unusual name. Any relation to the physicist Albert Baez?"

"He's my father," she answered. I told her that I admired him for his work as a physics teacher, although I had never met him. (I learned later that he had just been appointed to a faculty position at MIT, which is what put her in this part of the world.)

"And what do you do besides teach people how to ride Vespas?" I asked.

"I sing in a local club," she answered. She told me that it was Club 47, near Harvard (an unpaid job, as I learned later). I told her that I might stop by some time to hear her, but I never did. Even then, I had an aversion to cigarette smoke, which I imagined would be a principal ingredient of the Club 47 atmosphere.

With Joan hanging onto me, we made it safely back to the gas station, and I set out for Waltham on my own (without a helmet, of course).

It was only a year or two later that my Vespa instructor became famous, and before long I was one of her legions of devoted fans. Years later, I listened over and over to a tape of Joan singing folk songs in Spanish, a favorite as I steered my Volkswagen over long stretches of New Mexico highway. In 2007, Joan showed up for a concert near Philadelphia, and my wife, Joanne, and I joined the admiring throng in attendance.

When Joan held down her day job as a Vespa instructor, she was only seventeen. Here's what she had to say later about that job, in her memoir *Daybreak,* written when she was all of twenty-something: "Just before I made that money singing [her Club 47 exposure landed her a job in a Chicago nightclub that paid $400 for two weeks' work], I had the only legitimate job I've ever had outside of singing (which I've always felt was cheating). I taught people how to ride Vespa motor scooters. . . . I was paid a dollar and a quarter an hour for the most hair-raising job on the payroll, and eventually I quit because, a) I was going crazy from people who had no sense of balance, and b) I was offered the job singing in the nightclub."

Ken on the second Vespa, Newport Beach, California, 1965

Ercoupe, Santa Fe, New Mexico, 1953

Colorado River, Utah, 1953

Arches National Monument, Utah, 1953

Strahl Lake, Brown County State Park, Indiana, 1953

St. Peter's Dome, Jemez Mountains, New Mexico 1954

Valle Grande, New Mexico, 1954

Aboard MS Italia, September 1955

Near Bad Honnef, Germany, September 1955

Kleinwalsertal, Austria, March 1956

Karin, Ken, Nebelhorn, Oberstdorf, Germany, March 1956

Karin, Cambridge, England, April 1956

94D CROMWELL ROAD

I thank the residents of 94D Cromwell Road, London, where most of this book was written, for providing a pleasant working environment.

from the Foreword to *The World of Elementary Particles* (1963)

London was uniformly gray on that Saturday morning in September 1960. The sky seemed as close and as damp and as colorless as the buildings around me. Through the light fog, even the black taxis and the black umbrellas looked gray. If any pedestrians were sporting color, I didn't notice it.

I had arrived from Boston the previous day to spend a fellowship year at Imperial College working with Abdus Salam, head of the theoretical physics group at the College. I had met Abdus on one of his visits to America, and liked him. He had the twinkly eyes, ample girth, and sense of fun that might have suited him to play Santa Claus—had he not been a dark-skinned, dark-haired Pakistani and follower of Islam. At 35—the same age as I—he was already a senior professor and regular circuit rider to the scattered international outposts of physics. Later he would win the Nobel Prize for his interpretation of the forces between subnuclear particles. Abdus was married with children. I was just divorced, with children.

Upon arriving in London after an overnight flight, I tracked down a cheap hotel in the South Kensington district recommended in *Europe on Five Dollars a Day,* and checked in. After a nap and a bath, I walked to Imperial College to greet Abdus and get advice from his secretary on finding accommodations in the neighborhood. I met some of the other theorists, was shown the all-important tea room, and learned that Abdus had generously provided an office with three desks for me and the two students who would be joining me for the year. Now it was time to find a place to stay.

From an agency in Earl's Court I picked up information on available rooms to rent. Most were "bed sitting rooms" without cooking privileges. Some were shared apartments. I looked at a bed sitting room. Then I visited a large apartment on the second floor of 94 Cromwell Road, near the corner of Gloucester Road. This had been a three-story mansion before it was carved into apartments. Kathy, accompanied by her pre-school-age daughter, opened the door at 94D. She was an attractive woman in her late 20s, chosen by the apartment's owner to keep the rooms rented, collect the rent, and keep the place clean. The apartment had four large bedrooms, a living room, a spacious kitchen, a bathroom with a large tub (and plenteous hot water), and a separate WC. Kathy and her daughter occupied one bedroom, Mercedes another, and Michael another. The fourth room, in the back corner, was available. The rent fit within my limited budget. I said I would think about it.

Then I paced the streets. Being apart from my four-year-old son and two-year-old daughter was hard enough when they and I were in the same city. Now, finding myself suddenly three thousand miles away, I was hit with longing, not just for my children but also for friends and for all that was familiar. How should I structure this new life? Did I need the privacy of a bed sitting room? If I made that choice, I argued to myself, I would still have the companionship of my students and my physics colleagues. Did I need human company where I lived? Did I really want to get involved with a bunch of strangers? Wherever I lived, I knew that I would need time to write lots of letters and to start writing a book.

So I walked about in gray London. I had lunch at Blimpie's. I tried to visualize the coming year. Finally, the uncertainty of life in the shared apartment seemed less unsettling than the certainty of loneliness in a bed sitting room. I went back to Kathy and said I was ready to move in.

Kathy had moved into the apartment after her divorce from a husband whose ardor died on their wedding day. She worked as a secretary. Every morning she took her daughter, Anna, to her mother's apartment or to a day care center and every evening collected Anna, using buses and the Underground. Anna was a sweet, quiet child. Michael, about Kathy's age, was her boyfriend. They talked of marriage, but not too seriously. Michael was an office worker with a secondary-school education who aspired to become a gentleman, or at least middle-class. He wasn't sure that Kathy and Anna would be assets as he climbed the ladder he had in mind.

Mercedes—we called her Mercy—worked for a temp firm as a calculator operator assigned to one company after another. She was in her mid-30s, a delightful hedonist whose idea of the distant future was next week. She had quite an appetite for sex and liked to change men about as often as jobs. Within a few days of my arrival, she showed up in my room after dinner to chat me up. "What are you doing?" she asked.

"I'm trying to get started on a book."

"Amazing," she said. "I have a lot of friends who call themselves writers, but none of them actually writes."

She learned about my former life, my divorce, my children. I learned about her job as a calculator operator and about her origins outside of London. After a while, she evidently decided that I was not likely to end up in her bed. She left the room with a cheery good night, and we were buddies henceforth.

As life at 94D developed, Kathy, Mercy, and I formed a team. We shared shopping, cooking, and dishwashing duties. Michael joined us sometimes, but often came home late. Typically, Kathy and Anna and Mercy and I would gather for tea and sweets right after work. Then, following whatever personal things we had to do, such as letter writing or bill paying, we would gather again in the kitchen and cook dinner. After some conversation, we would split again. Pretty soon Mercy became chief shopper, Kathy chief cook, and I chief dishwasher.

How happy I soon was that I had chosen this apartment. I was fond of these people, and 94D was home. Occasionally one of my students came by in the evening to play recorder duets. Sometimes I went out to a movie. But in general, I felt contentment in the domesticity of the apartment. I was kept in a frame of mind that permitted me to work at my physics all day and write nearly every evening—chapters of the book and letters to my children.

We made our separate breakfasts, but often ate them together. Sometimes Kathy or Mercy would run downstairs for the mail and bring mine to me at the breakfast table. (The first of the day's three mail deliveries was before 8:00 a.m.)

Michael, growing restless, moved out not long after I moved in, but he came around to visit now and then. His room was taken by Andrew, who succumbed at once to Mercy's charms. They were best friends for several weeks. Andrew didn't stay long and never joined our "team." He was replaced by another man, who kept to himself.

About two months after Michael's departure, Kathy came shyly into my room one night in her nightgown (propelled there, I'm pretty sure, by Mercy). She stayed the night. And nights thereafter. So, for a time, I replaced Michael as Kathy's boyfriend. But it was Michael who had her heart. Perhaps her fling with me made her think harder about what she wanted in life, and made Michael (who was soon aware) think harder about what he might be losing. Less than a year later, after I was back in Boston, I heard from Michael and Kathy. They were married and were off to Perth to start a new life, with a generous government subsidy made available to those in Great Britain who emigrated to Australia. For a few years, we corresponded intermittently, and I sent them a copy of the book that was mostly written at 94D.

*　*　*　*　*

Temperature is one thing I hadn't reckoned with in London. My spacious room with its two outside walls seemed to violate one law of physics. It was colder than the outdoors. The room contained a kerosene heater, which vented its carbon monoxide and unburned fuel vapor back into the room.

When I first tried it in October, I awoke with a disagreeable headache. It took only two nights to convince me that this heater was not the solution to the chill. So I went out to Gloucester Road and bought an "electric fire," a heater with a curved reflector that beamed the heat in one direction. This got me through November and December and contributed to good posture. I positioned myself at my table to catch the radiation from the heater placed to one side of me on the floor. But the zone of warmth was narrow. If I leaned forward to squint at my paper or leaned backward to ponder, I left the heat zone, and had to quickly resume my original posture to regain the heat.

Using the excuse of the heating problem, but mostly because I wanted to act in what I considered the best interests of Michael and Kathy and Anna, I said farewell to my friends in January, and moved to the nearby Brompton House Hotel (another recommendation of *Europe on Five Dollars A Day),* where shillings fed into a gas heater (properly vented) kept me warm enough. Before long, Michael moved back into 94D, and I stopped by to see the gang now and then. Mercy found an Arab with staying power. She corralled him at the Gloucester Road Underground station, and they stuck together for quite a while. When, finally, he had to go back to his native country and his wife, he wrote letters and sent gifts. Mercy was almost in love.

In late February, I went off on a ski holiday to Wengen, Switzerland, and there I wrote the last few pages of *The World of Elementary Particles.* What Kathy and Mercy and Michael probably didn't know, but what I knew well, is that without them the book would not have been written so quickly, perhaps not written at all. They were warm friends at a critical time.

Ken, Schladming, Austria, March 1962

Wengen, Switzerland, February 1962

Ken, Kisters Field, Bloomington, Indiana, Spring 1957

Karin and George, Bloomington, Indiana, Spring 1957

Karin, Lake Peak, New Mexico, Summer 1957

Ken, Lake Peak, New Mexico, Summer 1957

Ken and Paul (~2 weeks), Los Alamos, New Mexico, 1957

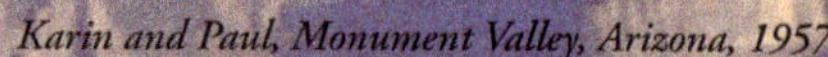

Karin and Paul, Monument Valley, Arizona, 1957

Karin and the Buick, Arizona, March 1958

Ercoupe, Window Rock, Arizona, 1958

BUILDING A GREAT UNIVERSITY
The UCI miracle

In the mid 1960s the state of California established three new universities almost simultaneously. They were planned and brought to life with astonishing skill and foresight and with astonishing levels of financial support. They were UC San Diego, opened for grad students in 1960 and undergraduates in 1964; UC Santa Cruz, opened for students at all levels in 1965; and UC Irvine, opened, like UCSC, for students at all levels in 1965. All became truly first-rate universities by any international standard.

Nothing like this had ever happened before, and I don't think anything like it has happened since (certainly not in the United States, although perhaps in China). It was something of a miracle— some combination, perhaps, of leadership in the already established university campuses such as UC Berkeley and UCLA; leadership in state government; bulging coffers; and a sense of optimism prevailing in the decades immediately following World War II. California's location on the west coast and the state's rapidly expanding population and economy very likely played a role, too. Manifest destiny had not faded from the American—especially the western American—conscience.

I was part of the Irvine miracle. I will write about that.

Here's how I got involved. In early1964—perhaps February or March—I got a call in my Brandeis Office from Ivan Hinderaker. He was then Chancellor of the UC Riverside campus and was helping to organize the planned UC Irvine campus. I don't recall what he told me about himself, only that he said he was recruiting for a physics department chair at a new UC campus, would be in the Boston area in the near future, and would like to talk to me to get suggestions for a possible person to fill that position. I was then department chair at Brandeis and had no thought whatsoever of moving elsewhere. I thought I might be able to help him on his mission and invited him to visit. A week or two later, Ivan showed up at my office and we repaired to the Brandeis cafeteria to talk while having coffee and a snack. He told me about Irvine and outlined what he was looking for: someone still young, perhaps around 37, with a record of accomplishment, a solid but not necessarily stellar researcher, a good teacher, someone with some administrative experience. He was precisely describing me, but it didn't occur to me that he was there to look me over. (You don't believe this, dear reader, but it's true. I took him at his word.) I could, in fact, think of two or three people that met his criteria, and I mentioned these names to him. He dutifully wrote down my suggestions, then asked, "How about you, Ken? Would you be interested?" I was nonplussed, stammered, and said, "well, maybe."

The "well, maybe" turned into a visit that spring to the windswept site of the Irvine campus, where construction was already under way. Joanne, although quite happy in our Wayland home where we had lived since our marriage less than two years earlier, was *semi*-supportive, *somewhat* encouraging. Before long I had a job offer. By that time Joanne knew she was pregnant (Adam arrived that December). We agreed to pull up stakes and embark on this new venture if we could delay our move to California until the following spring. For about nine months (July 1964 to March 1965) I would use our home in Wayland, Massachusetts as a base and travel, as needed, for recruiting, planning, and consultation. Irvine's Chancellor, Dan Aldrich, and Academic Vice Chancellor, Jack Peltason, agreed to this scheme, and it worked.

University of California, Irvine campus under construction, 1964

I used the adjective "astonishing" twice in the first paragraph. Here's what I was authorized to do (and did) in the first year, before students arrived.

- Hire six faculty
- Hire a senior secretary and two junior secretaries
- Hire a business manager
- Jointly with Chemistry, hire a machinist and a glass blower
- Set up a doctoral program under the wing of UCLA
- Recruit for graduate students and grant admission to some (a dozen arrived in the fall of 1965)
- Establish courses, both graduate and undergraduate, and assign faculty to teach them
- With Chemistry, purchase equipment for a machine shop
- With Chemistry, purchase equipment for a glass-blowing shop
- Work with architects and planners to specify future space needs for physics
- Purchase equipment for undergraduate labs

Regarding the last item in this list: A representative of Central Scientific (Cenco) made an appointment with Vice Chancellor Peltason to explain to him that UCI's new physics chair didn't understand how to set up a physics department. He (the Cenco rep) reported that the new chair was off ordering sophisticated equipment from various companies when he should be outfitting his student labs with Cenco equipment, like all well-run physics departments in the country did. When Jack Peltason asked me about this, I explained why I was doing what I was doing, and he backed me up. Cenco survived this insult, although it does now have numerous competitors, and no longer expects to be the automatic first choice.

2647 Basswood Street, Newport Beach, California, 1965

What was the benefit of all of this? First and foremost, the recognition by prospective new faculty members that UCI had the resources and the commitment to achieve major-university status in a hurry. Several of the new physics faculty members were already leaders in their field, and others were recommended as having extraordinary potential. It was only our rocket launch that persuaded them to join the new enterprise.

I did not advertise for faculty nor review applications. Instead, I consulted with leaders in various fields—solid-state physics, particle physics, plasma physics, low-temperature physics, nuclear physics—and asked these leaders to recommend candidates, both senior and junior. It worked. Outstanding people accepted our offers ("our" meaning mine, reviewed by and endorsed by Jack Peltason and, in a few cases, by other already committed faculty). The initial seven-person department grew in its second year to fifteen. When Joanne and I returned to UCI in 2015 for its fiftieth anniversary celebration, the physics faculty numbered more than fifty. In the same half century, student enrollment grew from about 1,500 to about 30,000. And, needless to say, buildings proliferated. Without guidance I would have been lost on the 2015 campus.

On a wintry day in March 1965, Joanne and I, with five-year-old Nina, two-year-old Caroline, and three-month-old Adam set off from Wayland, Massachusetts in a VW bus headed for our new home in Newport Beach, California. On one of my trips to UCI, I had contracted to buy a new home in a brand-new subdivision called Eastbluff. We stretched to meet the $40,000 cost of the home, one of the largest and most expensive in Eastbluff. (Our Wayland home, with its two acres of land, sold for a bit over half that amount.) Our two other children, Paul and Sarah, would spend summers with us, and who knew how many other little ones would later join the family. We needed the space.

Joanne, Caroline, and Nina part way across the country, 1965

With the first students scheduled to arrive on the first of October, we had time to get acquainted with other early staff—chairs, deans, top administrators, and some support staff. It was a pleasant period. We liked to joke later that that first year, with no students, was the best year of all. There was indeed one "best" about it—the chance to interact with brilliant, mostly young, leaders in fields far removed from physics. We organized seminars, affording me a once-in-a-life time chance to deliver a talk on physics research to an audience of chemists, biologists, humanists, social scientists, and an artist. That first-year group included 34-year-old James (Jim) McGaugh, who became a world-renowned and much-honored neurobiologist; and 37-year-old Sherwood (Sherry) Rowland, who went on to win the 1995 Nobel Prize in Chemistry.

Not surprisingly, our Eastbluff neighborhood attracted other faculty members. Our immediate neighbors on one side were Seymour Menton, a scholar of Spanish literature, and his wife, Kathy. A little later, Fred Reines and his wife, Sylvia, moved into the house on the other side. Our children loved Fred. (In 1995 he joined Sherry Rowland in Stockholm, where he was awarded the Nobel Prize in Physics.) Eastbluff was no more than two miles from the campus. Its location and Orange County's agreeable climate encouraged me to buy another Vespa motor scooter (as I had done at Brandeis—see "Joan's Job"). It got me back and forth between home and office.

Just six years later, we were drawn back to the east, after two more children joined the family—Jason in Costa Mesa, California in 1966 and Lucas in Los Alamos, New Mexico in 1968. (A vasectomy a few weeks before Lucas's birth assured that he would be the last.) For me, the UCI job was the highlight of my professional (non-writing) career: exciting, rewarding, satisfying, fun. Even

Caroline, Ken, Paul, Sarah, and Nina in the backyard of 2647 Basswood Street, Newport Beach, California, 1965

for Joanne, for whom southern California was an alien land, there are good memories—child rearing and friendships, including with Joan Rowland and Rita Mayer, both of whom lived in nearby Corona del Mar; and with immediate Eastbluff neighbors: Kathy Menton on one side, Sylvia Reines on the other.

Yet we did leave. Joanne had gone to college in Boston, worked in that area, married in that area, had three children in that area. That's where her heart was. Once UCI was well launched, I agreed to return, and a job offer from U Mass Boston made that possible.

I still stand in awe of California's visionary leaders, both educational and political.

Ken, Jackson Hole, Wyoming, April 1966

THE '60S

The twentieth century's most significant decade

In the late 1960s, I was walking across the Berkeley campus of the University of California when I encountered a crowd of students running toward me. When I sniffed the teargas, I knew why they were running, and I joined them until we were in the clear. I never did find out what they had been protesting against: whether the Vietnam War, racial injustice, or perhaps the policy of giving grades.

At the time I was a physics professor at another UC campus, located in Irvine (see "Building a Great University"). There we experienced less turbulence than at Berkeley, and never resorted to teargas, although the students did, at one time, occupy the Chancellor's office. I got into the spirit of the times by wearing blue work shirts and letting my hair grow. When I joined an antiwar candlelight vigil, I felt daring. At a faculty party, Joanne and I were offered marijuana in lieu of dessert. We politely declined.

For some reason, I got elected to chair the Faculty Senate. In that role, I learned that the faculty, unlike the students, were split right down the middle, half embracing activism, half rejecting it. Some of those who embraced it raised enough money to send one person to Washington to express our point of view to our Congressman. I got chosen. Representative Utt listened politely to me. Nothing he did or said later suggested that my pitch had had any effect. After my visit to his office, since I had a bit of extra time, I joined an antiwar march before heading to the airport.

Sarah, Nina, Caroline, Paul, and Adam, Newport Beach, California, 1965

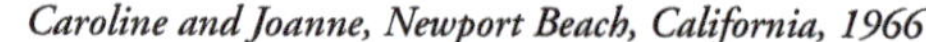

Caroline and Joanne, Newport Beach, California, 1966

OATHS, SIGNED AND UNSIGNED

Resistance to authority

Ken, Dulles International Airport, October 25, 1973

I am wanted in Massachusetts. My crime, committed many years ago, was refusing to sign a loyalty oath. You won't find my face on a Wanted poster in any Post Office. No, the record of my offense lies deep in a file drawer in the Massachusetts Superior Court. It will probably stay there forever.

In 1971, after six years in Newport Beach, California, my wife, Joanne, was longing for her beloved New England. What had brought us to Newport Beach was the Irvine campus of the University of California (see "Building a Great University"). I had come to that new campus to set up its physics department, and I was more than happy there. Nevertheless, with UCI well launched, I decided to scan the eastern horizon in search of—as the saying goes—new opportunities. I was offered a professorship at the Boston campus of the University of Massachusetts, and accepted it. No one mentioned that I would be required to sign a State loyalty oath as a condition of employment.

We loaded children, luggage, and cat into our Volkswagen bus and headed for Los Alamos, New Mexico, where I was to spend an interim year working on a textbook and guiding the work of a graduate student. Then it was on to Massachusetts. I checked out my new office, greeted my colleagues, and headed across campus to the Personnel Office. There I was presented with miscellaneous forms to sign—payroll, health insurance, retirement, and—whoops!—a State loyalty oath. I hadn't reckoned on that. This stale residue of anti-Communist fervor was still on the books, still required of every public employee—everyone who worked for State, county, or township; every trash collector, public librarian, and U Mass professor.

Once, years before, when Senator Joseph McCarthy was pervasively and perniciously influential, I had been presented with another loyalty oath to sign, that one from the state of California. I didn't like it and didn't want to sign it, but I did. I'll come back to that. In 1972, in Massachusetts, I didn't intend to capitulate again.

What to do? In a letter to the University president I explained why I didn't want to sign the oath. (The rationale I offered was only part of the story. I'll come back to that, too.) The president could do nothing. I talked it over with some Quaker friends. They supported my position. My faculty colleagues, on the other hand, regarded the oath as a nuisance or a joke, perhaps even a bit of an embarrassment for the State, but not worth getting excited about.

Time passed. I started teaching. I got paid. Soon I learned that just two other University employees, a young man and a young woman, both clerical workers, had refused to sign the oath. They had also started work and were being paid. The University was not as efficient as it should have been in screening out malcontents like us before letting us go to work. I met these two kindred spirits. We got a little publicity in the campus newspaper and the *Boston Globe,* but the loyalty oath was no longer an issue to stir passion.

The University, doing its duty, reported out intransigence to State authorities. Within a few months, our court case was scheduled—not, as I had expected, before a lower court, but directly before the Massachusetts Superior Court. In the meantime, our modest notoriety had brought us to the attention of a liberal attorney at a large Boston law firm. He was sufficiently offended by the oath requirement that he volunteered to represent us at no charge.

On the appointed day, my new friends and I dressed in what in my family we call our party clothes and went to court. Besides our attorney, we were accompanied by Elizabeth Boardman, a proper and prominent Quaker lady, who came along to lend moral support. As we sat waiting for the judge to appear, I was nervous—not at the prospect of the hearing but at the prospect that Elizabeth, in the spirit of her Quaker principles, might decline to stand when the judge entered the chamber. If she remained seated, I wondered, should I do the same? I turned and whispered, "Elizabeth, do you plan to stand when the judge comes in?"

"I like to make people happy," she whispered back. "If my standing makes the judge happy, I will stand."

That settled, I relaxed. The judge appeared, and we stood. There was some formal back and forth between the judge and the attorney. Although we miscreants had rehearsed the little speeches we would make when we were asked why we refused to sign the oath, we never got the chance to deliver them. We were asked only to state our names and our positions, truthfully. The closest I came to expressing an opinion about oaths was in response to the question "Do you swear to tell the truth, the whole truth, and nothing but the truth?" I answered, "I so *affirm.*"

It was over in minutes. The judge didn't express an opinion, but I couldn't help feeling that he didn't much like the loyalty oath law and just wanted it to go away. He knew that Massachusetts was only one of many states that had adopted or expanded loyalty-oath laws when irrational fear of Communists clouded clear thinking. And he knew that the legislatures in most of the other states had, by this time, come to their senses and repealed such laws. The judge couldn't make the Massachusetts law go away, but it was in his power to make our case go away. He directed that the case be postponed until such time as it pleased the court to reopen it. As we left the courtroom, I asked our attorney how long that might be. "There's a good chance," he answered, "that your case will never be tried. This judge obviously doesn't like the loyalty oath. He is burying your case, and it's unlikely ever to be exhumed."

I marveled at the judge's power. I and my fellow defendants congratulated each other. We thanked the attorney. We thanked Elizabeth Boardman. We went back to work. It's been a great many years, and I have never quite forgotten that somewhere, at the back of some file drawer in Boston, there is a piece of paper that says that I am "wanted."

Now, why *did* I refuse to sign the loyalty oath? What I told the press and was prepared to tell the judge was that I viewed the oath requirement as an exercise of arbitrary authoritarian power designed to stifle dissent, to intimidate those who would freely express their views, to plant seeds of fear in the minds of citizens. To me it was one step on a road to thought control. True freedom is a precious gift that is easily eroded. Protecting it requires endless vigilance. But these arguments of principle were not the whole story. I had to admit that I was, in my own way, a rebel (see "Rebellion").

* * * * *

Yet the first time I confronted a loyalty oath, I didn't put my job on the line, as I later did in Massachusetts. In 1950 I had a more flexible backbone. I was twenty-four and had interrupted my graduate studies at Princeton to join a theoretical physics group at Los Alamos Laboratory in New Mexico. Since the University of California managed the lab for the Atomic Energy Commission, everyone who worked at the lab was an employee of that university. At this time, the long shadow of Senator Joseph McCarthy lay across the land. In California the University Regents acted to require all University employees to sign an oath of loyalty to the State of California and to the United

States. Faculty resistance in California was strong. At Berkeley and other campuses, some of the finest professors quit. But at Los Alamos, the oath sailed through the lab with scarcely a ripple. All but two of the lab's 3,000 or so staff members signed the oath—many of them, to be sure, appending written protests.

The two who did not sign were John Manley and I. Manley was an associate director of the lab, a respected senior scientist, a veteran of the Manhattan Project. I was the most junior of junior scientists. I wrote a letter to Norris Bradbury, the director of the lab, explaining why I did not want to sign the oath. Among my reasons: I had never set foot in California and couldn't see the logic of defending its constitution. Bradbury called me into his office. "Ken," he said, "I understand how you feel. I completely agree with your sentiments. But my hands are tied. There is nothing I can do. If you don't sign the oath, I have to terminate your employment." That was straightforward enough. I had to weigh the pros and cons—my principles (and my rebelliousness) against what I could accomplish in the job and would gain from the notable scientists I would be working with. When the guillotine was about to fall, I signed.

John Manley did not sign. He left the lab to become the Chair of the physics department of the University of Washington in Seattle. He was my hero. Forty-five years later, in 1995, in connection with a book I was working on, I called Manley's widow to get her perspective on the oath. "Is it true," I asked, "that John refused on principle to sign the oath and therefore had to leave the lab?"

"Gracious no," she answered. "It's true that he was opposed to the oath, but not so opposed that he would have risked his job. He already had an offer from the University of Washington, which he planned to accept. Since he was leaving the lab anyway, he saw no reason to sign the oath." It was too late to talk to Manley to get his version, but I do know that after the University of California rescinded its oath requirement, Manley returned from Washington to the Los Alamos Lab and spent the rest of his career there. I prefer to think of him as a hero.

Well, dear reader, that's the story of my resistance to loyalty oaths. Make of it what you will. Perhaps from this tale you will come to understand me better than I understand myself.

Ken, Silver Spring, Maryland, 1982

CHILD'S PLAY

It can be scary

I used to love being physical with my children, and they loved it, too. Not just hugging and holding, but rough-and-tumble activities. They never tired of riding on my shoulders, clutching my hair in a mixture of fear and joy as I pretended to be a trotting horse. Another favorite was for a child to take my two hands in her two hands, facing me, then climbing up until her feet were straight up and her head straight down, finally flipping to complete a loop and landing on her feet. "More, Daddy. More. Just once more!"

Then there was getting me down on the floor and squealing happily as they jumped up and down on me as if I were a feather bed. Some of the children enjoyed being tossed straight up and being caught on the way down, but some didn't. Not every child can cope with the feeling of weightlessness, the feeling of being cut off from support.

One favorite of all of the children was being an airplane. I would take, say, a child's left wrist and left ankle in my two hands and twirl around, alternately raising the child as high as I could manage and swooping down to within inches of the ground as we went around. I got dizzy before the child did. This stunt needed space. I usually did it outside.

Once Jason asked me in the living room if he could be an airplane. I obliged. We went around and around, up and down, and when I set him back on his feet, I noticed that the whirling had carried his head to within inches of the corner of a heavy wooden coffee table.

There's a saying for such a moment: A chill runs down your spine. It's accurate. I felt a chill. Sweat broke out on my forehead. I had to sit down. I don't think Jason noticed that anything was amiss. I hope not. At that instant, the event was engraved in my memory. I would like to erase that engraving, but I can't. It's now more than forty years later, and I still sometimes wake up in in the night, having just dreamed that Jason's head didn't miss the coffee table. There is such a thing as a cold sweat. I know it.

Jason and Ken, Chaco Culture Historical Park, New Mexico, 1968

Henry and Elizabeth Kolm, Joanne, and Edith, Weir Meadow, Wayland, Massachusetts, 1961

Joanne, Nina, Sarah, and Paul, Weir Meadow, Wayland, Massachusetts, 1961

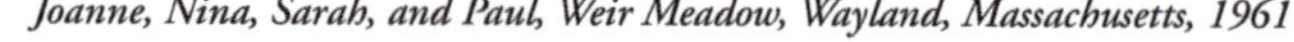

Volkswagens, Weir Meadow, Wayland, Massachusetts, 1962

Ken, Jungfraujoch, Switzerland, February 1962   *Ken and Joanne, Green Cay, St. Croix, May 1962*

Joanne and Ken on their wedding day, Red Lodge, Wayland, Massachusetts, June 9, 1962

Lawrence Baumunk and Joanne, Wayland, Massachusetts, June 9, 1962

Joanne, Edith, Ken, and Caroline Baumunk, Red Lodge, Wayland, Massachusetts, June 9, 1962

Ken, Mt. Katahdin, Maine, June 1962

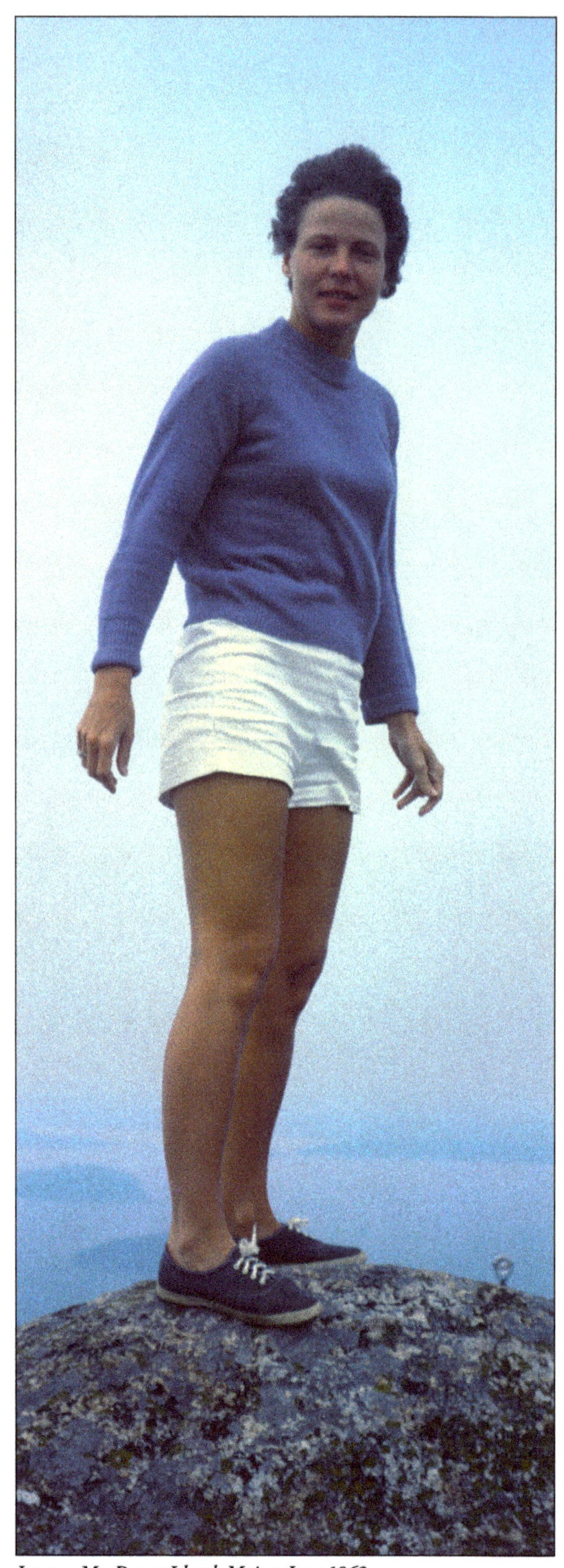

Joanne, Mt. Desert Island, Maine, June 1962

Joanne, Mt. Desert Island, Maine, June 1962

Joanne, Moosehead Lake, Maine, June 1962

REGRETS

Big and small, they stay with you

Elizabeth Taylor was married eight times, and had no regrets. Harry Truman authorized the use of atomic weapons against Japan and had no regrets. Lucky them. My middle name is Regrets. My life is strewn with actions that I regret. Some are big, like changing jobs too often. One is beyond big, getting divorced. Some are middle-sized, like leaving a teaching job that I loved just because I was 72. Some are small, like not offering to share my motel room in California with a young German couple for whom there was no room at the inn. That incident with the Germans was in 1999, and it still bothers me. "Why didn't I think more quickly? Why wasn't I more hospitable?" I ask myself. Regret over small actions has a bad habit of burrowing into one's brain and taking residence there, alongside the big ones.

Take Tar. Tar was a big black dog—friendly, intelligent, young enough to be rambunctious. He was a mixture of Lab and Collie. He was about a year old when he joined our family in Weston, Massachusetts, a Boston suburb where dogs could run free. We all loved Tar. Ten-year-old Adam and twelve-year-old Caroline, especially, loved Tar.

In 1975, when Tar was two, I accepted a job as president of New Mexico Tech and we prepared, once again, to move (see "On Being a College President"). Our oldest child, Paul, 17, was a senior in boarding school and would stay

Tar, Weston, Massachusetts, 1973

in the east for college. The next two, Sarah, 16, and Nina, also 16, would be left behind as well, enrolled in two other boarding schools. The children who would accompany us to New Mexico that summer would be Caroline, 12, Adam, 10, Jason, 8, and Lucas, 6. But what about Tar? Could we manage to transport him?

We decided that Caroline and I would be the scouting party. She and I would drive west in our Volkswagen bug and check out the town, the campus, and the president's house. Then we would fly back to Massachusetts, from where the whole family—my wife, Joanne, plus the four younger children and I—would set out together in our Volkswagen bus for the four-day trip to our new home. Tar posed the toughest dilemma. He was a big dog. Was it practical to shoehorn him into a vehicle full of six people and a lot of luggage? The images of Clifford, the large red dog in a series of children's books, came to mind. Joanne and I agonized over this question. Finally, we decided that the answer was No. Tar, much as we loved him, would have to stay in Massachusetts and make a new home with a new family. Here's more to regret: We didn't tell Adam and Caroline what we were up to.

We advertised in a local paper, and agreed to give Tar to a family who contacted us. Two men came in a van. Tar was suspicious. He sensed that something not to his liking was about to happen. It took three of us to get him into the van. When the van, with Tar in it, disappeared down the street, my eyes were

Adam and Tar, Weston, Massachusetts, 1973

damp, and so were Joanne's. We embraced and went into the house. Then I heard sobbing. There were Caroline and Adam, looking out the window of his bedroom, holding each other and sobbing. They were caught unaware.

Comforting these two wasn't easy, since Joanne and I ourselves felt the need to be comforted. Eventually they stopped crying, and we had a somber supper, trying to be upbeat about the new

Adam and Tar, Weston, Massachusetts, 1973

life ahead in New Mexico. The other children, who took Tar's loss more in stride, lightened the supper-table mood a little. I couldn't help thinking, "Did we make a terrible mistake? Should we have found a way, somehow, to take Tar with us?" And the worst question of all to think about, "Have we done irreparable harm to the children's psyches?"

Adam says now that the day we gave Tar away no longer stands out in his memory. Caroline remembers it well. And for me, there it is, as vivid as ever. I would like to forget it, but I can't.

ON BEING A COLLEGE PRESIDENT
NMIMT

In the spring of 1975, just after I turned 49, I was getting ready to leave my job as chair of the physics department at U Mass Boston and move to Socorro, NM, to take up a new job as president of New Mexico Tech. This college (or university) was founded in the 1880s as the New Mexico School of Mines. In 1951 it transmuted into New Mexico Institute of Mining and Technology. Now, because mining accounts for only a small part of its programs of education and research, it is most commonly called just New Mexico Tech. As I was gathering up belongings from my office, I said to my secretary, "May I have the New Mexico Tech folder."

"It's all here," she said as she handed it to me, "right from your first letter saying you were not interested."

I can't now remember who nominated me for the job, nor can I remember just what switched me from not being interested to being interested. I do remember being interviewed by four of the college's five Regents. They came to Boston (possibly on a trip that involved meeting more than one candidate). I picked them up at their hotel in our VW bus on a Sunday morning. We drove to the U Mass campus to talk in an unused conference room. I supplied coffee and donuts. Missing from the meeting was Regent Jamie Woods. After I arrived in Socorro that summer, and after Jamie and I became friends, he confided to me that he had declined to accompany his fellow Regents to Boston because he "wasn't going to fly across the country just to visit another damned physicist." (Jamie Woods, like me, was a pilot. He even allowed me to fly his plane on occasion, when I needed one that would hold six instead of four.) The physicist who failed to inspire him was Tech's then-president, Stirling Colgate. (Stirling, as his last name suggests, was not poor. It was said by his peers in the physics community, "Stirling wanted to be a college president, so he bought a college.")

After that interview in Boston, I traveled to Socorro for more interviewing and to meet faculty and staff. Before long I was offered the job, and I liked the prospect. Joanne was certainly not keen on the move, yet she agreed to go—perhaps because she sensed my lack of real enthusiasm for U Mass Boston; perhaps because she knew too well that her husband, at this stage of his life, craved new challenges; perhaps because New Mexico was not California. We had enjoyed our two stints in Los Alamos. (We had enjoyed California, too, and had good friends there, but Joanne wanted to get back to her friends in the east.)

So, in June 1975, the advance party—Ken, aged 49, and Caroline, aged 12—headed west in our VW beetle. A lovely cross-country drive, with open windows playing the role of air conditioner. Caroline kept a meticulous log of every town and hamlet on the trip, checking them off as we passed through. Parts of her log, including the New Mexico portion, are pictured here.

For the first weeks in Socorro, we "roughed it," with beds but no other furniture. It was during that time, before the rest of the family joined us, that Caroline wrote and illustrated a children's book, *Jane.* It's a charming book that was published many years later.

One remembers odd things. I remember that on our first night in Socorro, I woke in the middle of the night needing a blanket, although it had been agreeably warm at bedtime. And I remember my first day on the job, with a superb inherited secretary, Lucy Chavez. I asked Lucy how she pronounced her last name. She said, "Well, you gringos call it cha-VEZZ; I call it CHA-vess." I knew we would get along.

My memory of that summer of 1975 is a little vague. Caroline and I must have flown back to Massachusetts. Then all of us—Joanne and I and our five youngest children—and a good deal of luggage squeezed into a VW bus and headed west. I can't remember what route we took or how many days we were on the road. In any event, we settled easily in the very adequate house (with swimming pool) provided by the Institute.

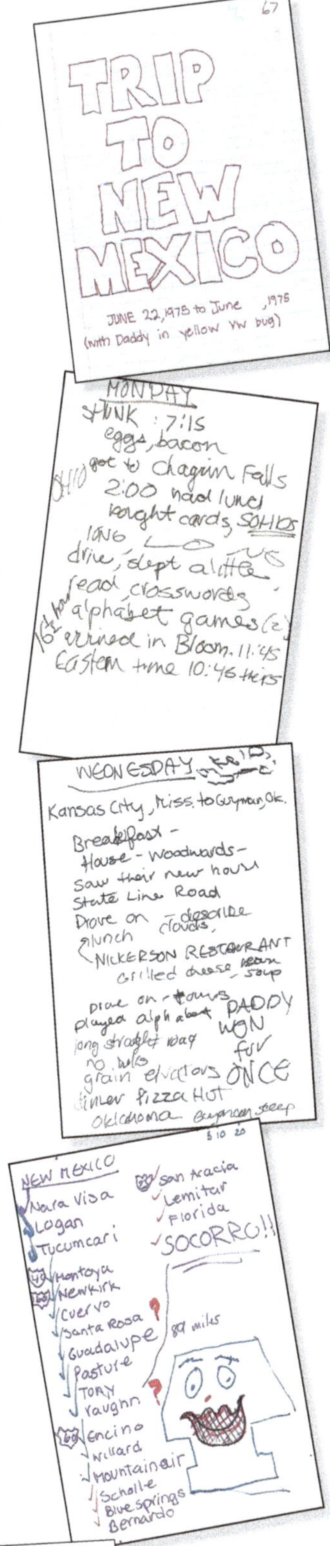

*   *   *   *   *

Of the foolish assumptions I made upon taking on the responsibility of a college president, surely the most foolish was the assumption that I would easily gain the support of faculty and students because I had, after all, been a successful faculty colleague and teacher for years. And I thought, also foolishly, that I knew how to select good people because I had done so successfully at UC Irvine. I needed professional advice on "how to be a college president." But I didn't know I needed guidance and I didn't seek it.

My vote of no confidence came after six years of service, my resignation after seven. A vote of no confidence comes about not because a myopic faculty is unable to recognize one's merit and one's achievements. It comes about because it is deserved.

The qualities needed to successfully head a university are no different from those needed to successfully head a corporation: to appoint senior staff of excellence and to offer a vision that inspires everyone to pitch in. I had a mixed record in the first of these requirements (some super stars, some duds) and was less than stellar in the second.

I was, at least, aware of the need to work with varied constituencies. The college president has more of them than does the corporate executive. They include:

Ken on a Marathon Oil platform

- faculty
- students
- staff members
- alumni
- governing body (called Regents in New Mexico)
- townspeople (merchants, public-school officials, and citizens generally)
- State legislators (for a State-funded institution, as we were)
- fellow presidents and top officials at other State-supported institutions
- government granting agencies if one relies on outside research funding, as we did
- other sources of private funding

I did not work hard enough at faculty relations, but was reasonably successful with the other constituencies. (Students hardly count as a separate constituency, especially at a small, intimate university like New Mexico Tech where student attitudes largely track faculty attitudes.)

Shortly after my arrival, I succeeded in getting funding for what came to be called the Petroleum Recovery Research Center, an entity that still prospers. This was mostly the work of a Regent, John Kelly, who lived in Roswell and was in the oil business. I watched him "arm wrestle" Governor Jerry Apodaca at a reception in Santa Fe. He convinced the Governor that a few hundred thousand uncommitted dollars stashed away in some State account might as well serve as seed money for a new research center at Tech. The rest, including a building, was up to the Legislature. So the PRRC came into existence, and we had the good fortune to hire Joe Taber, a professor at the University of Pittsburgh, to serve as its first director. Among the other outstanding staff he added was Lynn Orr, soon to become my flying buddy (and later a Stanford professor).

My predecessor had not paid much attention to "capital projects"—i.e., buildings. But we needed some buildings. (It is said of college presidents that they tend to develop an edifice complex.) At the top of my building wish list had to be the petroleum research center. It was promptly funded and built. Next on that list was a new gym, which was also funded and built. No one

New Mexico Tech gym construction, 1975

objected to the research center building, and almost no one to the gym ("I *like* the open-air racket ball courts," said one faculty member). What was next on the list after that was a combined theater and conference center. It was completed late in my tenure at Tech, and almost everyone objected to it. (Soon after it was completed, someone spray-painted on its wall, "Ford's Folly.") It's my understanding that now almost everyone—town and gown alike—approves of it.

* * * * *

Before my arrival at Tech, money to run the school was almost all government money—State and Federal. Private fund raising had been limited to routine annual solicitation from alumni. In my fifth year at Tech, I was able to gain approval in our budget for a professionally staffed fund-raising office. That staff consisted of one development officer and one secretary. To fill the development officer position we hired Don Salmon, who came from a fund-raising position at Regis College in Denver and was ready to run his own operation. I still remember something Don said to us when he was in Socorro for an interview: "One thing you should know about me is that I drive Cadillacs, the biggest and fanciest models I can find." I liked his directness. Don turned out to be as fine a person as I have ever worked with.

One thing Don could zero in on was alumni with means. One such was R. Gene Samples, the head of Consolidation Coal, who made a generous gift. Don and I visited him at his office in Pittsburgh, where he offered to help us raise money from other executives. Over lunch he twisted the arm of the president of Joy Manufacturing (a company that made heavy equipment for mining operations), securing a fairly handsome gift. The next morning, he loaded us into his corporate helicopter—along with hot coffee, fresh pastries, and morning newspapers—and we flew under low ceilings to New York, landing at a heliport on the East River in midtown Manhattan for appointments with two corporate executives. One of them was George Munroe, CEO of Phelps Dodge. He provided us with a good lunch, some nice copper souvenirs, and a

Ken, New Mexico Tech commencement, 1979

modest gift to Tech. The only thing I specifically remember our host saying was, "Too bad there isn't a market for copper foil the way there is for aluminum foil." We were back in Pittsburgh that evening.

Another very agreeable Tech alumnus, George Atwood, headed Duval Corporation, which mined and processed copper ore in Cochise County, Arizona. I don't remember the size of his gift, but I do remember that he was deeply interested in the chemistry of copper ore processing, and gave us a personal tour of his company's facilities.

An alumnus with whom Don Salmon struck up a personal friendship was Bill Macey, an "oil man." Our first visit with him was in Ruidoso, New Mexico, where he and his wife Jean had a house in addition to their homes in Denver and Tucson (which, in due course, we also visited). Don and I flew into Ruidoso's high-elevation and not overly long airstrip (it's longer now).

I must digress for a moment to say that Don was a wonderfully good sport about flying hither and yon in four-seat Cessnas, Bonanzas, and Mooneys. Actually, he says that he enjoyed the flying, and that he respected my skill and my caution as a pilot. In any case, we made a good team, aloft and on the ground. I do recall one flight that may have tested his respect for this mode of travel. On the above-mentioned trip to Pittsburgh to see Gene Samples, we stopped in Mountainair, New Mexico to pick up two young ladies and their luggage and their dog. The dog sat on a lap in the rear and gave the back of Don's neck a friendly lick. Why pick up passengers? New Mexico's official per-mile reimbursement rate for private planes, although greater than the rate for private automobiles, still fell short of the actual cost of flying, so I sometimes advertised for share-the-expense passengers—a practice I had started back in Massachusetts.

Over lunch in Ruidoso, Don explained our need for private funds to supplement State funding. "What are some of your present needs?" asked Bill. "Scholarships for needy students," answered Don. Bill pulled out a checkbook, wrote a check for $10,000, and handed it to Don. "Will that help?" he asked. Although impressed by this act of spontaneous generosity, I was perhaps even more impressed by the thought that anyone should keep more than ten thousand dollars in a checking account. Mine never exceeded a few hundred.

Not too much later, Don and I flew over to Tucson, where Bill Macey picked us up at the airport and took us to his home for dinner with himself and Jean. After dinner, Don described the theater-conference center that we hoped to build and he presented a written proposal. As I recall, the State Legislature had agreed to provide $2 million toward its estimated cost—which was closer to $3 million—provided we could raise the rest privately. On the spot, Bill and Jean agreed to donate $600,000 (this number I do remember). Don and I had agreed that if the Maceys donated at that level, we would propose to name the center for them. Don at once made this suggestion. Bill said, "No, no, there's no reason. We don't need such publicity." Jean said, "Oh, I think that would be lovely." It became Macey Center and, Ford's folly or not, remains a great asset to the campus and the town.

Another big infusion to this building's cost came from merchants in Socorro. A local fund drive headed by Holm Bursum, Jr., the town's leading banker, had a target of $125,000 and netted about $175,000. It was a pleasure seeing Holm work his persuasive powers on local business owners.

Macey Center, New Mexico Tech, 1981

After my departure (and Don's) from New Mexico Tech, Bill and Jean Macey remained generous donors to the school; and Holm Bursum, Jr. and his son, Holm III (another pilot) continued to be staunch supporters.

*　*　*　*　*

Socorro was not all fund raising and academic planning and constituencies. It was also the Ford family—the rather sizeable Ford family. In our first summer in Socorro, in 1975, the three older children—Paul, Sarah, and Nina—were 18, 16, and 16. Caroline, in the middle, was (as noted above) 12, and the three younger ones—Adam, Jason, and Lucas—were 10, 9, and 7. Joanne was a bit north of forty and Ken was just shy of 50.

New Mexico Tech President's house pool, winter 1978

As things worked out, our seven years in Socorro were, for the family, mostly a happy time. We were less than delighted with the public schools, but in the end the children gained good educations. And summers in Shunk were the norm. In 1975—our first Socorro year—Paul had just graduated from Exeter and was about to go to Princeton; Sarah and Nina were preparing to enroll in boarding schools—Sarah in Choate Rosemary Hall, Nina in Concord Academy. Caroline completed her high-school education in Socorro, and the younger boys eventually graduated from private schools—Adam from Concord Academy in 1983, Jason from Concord Academy in 1984, and Lucas from Germantown Friends School in 1986.

I can no longer remember which children spent how much time with us in Socorro. And I can only dimly remember road trips to sites within New Mexico and to Colorado. I just recall that we had some good times together, at home and on the road.

1 Olive Lane, Socorro, New Mexico, 1980

Joanne's focus was on children—not just our own but also those in the town. She read to preschoolers at the library and she helped establish a playground that still bears her name. One year we sent Jason to a small local private school, the Arcadia School. For Lucas, together with two children from family friends, Joanne created the Workshop School and more or less followed a Calvert curriculum developed for home-schoolers. The College's lawyer assured us that it was OK to open a private school in our College-owned house provided we met the state's three requirements: students from more than one family, an available fire extinguisher, and a door that swung out. (This lawyer added, "Just don't hold religious services in your house." We chose not to mention the biweekly Quaker worship groups that we hosted.) After one year in the Workshop School, Lucas attended public grade school. He was ready for middle school when we left Socorro for Maryland in 1982.

WRITE IT DOWN
Theme: Panic

"It sounds like you've been having panic attacks," said the counselor. I was so relieved, I almost laughed out loud. I had to explain to him why I was happy with this diagnosis. I had been afraid that I was suffering from the early onset of Alzheimer's or was in the grip of some other dread ailment.

I was the head of the American Institute of Physics at the time (it was around 1988) and I had to attend a lot of meetings, sometimes chairing them, sometimes not. A couple of months earlier I had begun to notice an odd thing, that at unpredictable times during meetings my mind would go blank. It was more likely to happen, I noticed, if it was a large meeting—a dozen or more people in the room—and if I was not the chair. I might raise my hand to speak and then have no idea what I wanted to say. Or I might say "Let me bring up three issues" and have no idea what the second and third ones were after I had stated the first one. Soon I tried to say as little as possible whenever I wasn't the chair and thus wasn't working from a written agenda. Sometimes, though, I got called on or was obviously expected to contribute an idea. Then my confusion was evident. Twice I had to say, "Please excuse me. I'm suffering from a dizzy spell," after which I got up and walked unsteadily from the room, returning in ten minutes or so, apparently recovered. This avoided too much embarrassment and too much gossip, since my colleagues knew that I had previously suffered from something called Menière's disease, an affliction of the inner ear that brings on the symptoms of seasickness and nausea without warning. But I couldn't go on pretending. I was worried. I knew I had to do something.

I talked the problem over with Terri Braun, my Director of Human Resources, whom I would call a motherly woman except that she was younger than I. Let's say she was sisterly. I trusted her judgment and trusted her discretion. She recommended an internist in New York. I visited him. He listened to my heart and lungs and administered an EKG, and we talked. "Nothing wrong with you that I can see," he said. "Let me recommend a neurologist."

So I went to the neurologist. He tapped my kneecaps and the soles of my feet with his rubber hammer, administered some tests of eye and hand coordination, fired questions at me from a prepared list, and we talked.

"Nothing neurologically wrong that I can see," he said. "I think your problem may be psychological, not physical. Let me recommend a counselor."

So I went to the counselor, and we talked. After he rendered his diagnosis and I expressed my relief, I asked, "So what should I do?"

His first suggestion was that I visit his office weekly and sit in a semi-dark room listening to soft music while trying to relax totally. I tried that once and only felt restless and uncomfortable. It was a very long hour. "For this I should pay money?" I asked myself.

His second suggestion was that I should take a pencil and pad to every meeting and take notes—notes of what others were saying, and, more important, notes of what I was thinking and what I might say. "If you have three points to make," he said, "write 1, 2, 3 on your pad, and put maybe only a single word after each number to trigger your recollection and remove the fear that you will forget. Anxiety is based on fear. Remove the fear."

What wonderful advice. It worked like magic. He had earned his fee. I didn't begrudge him the cost of my hour of gentle music in a dark room.

So ended the anxiety attacks. As time passed, I pretty much forgot about them. But the pencil and pad remained my constant companions at meetings. Some years later, after my retirement, I was reminiscing with a former colleague about those days.

"Weren't you quite ill at that time?" he asked. I had to think a moment.

"Oh," I said, "that's right. I was."

Ken, Wayland, Massachusetts, 1964

My Life as a "With-Author"

John Wheeler's life takes shape

A child, when asked "What do you want to be when you grow up?" might answer a fireman or a policeman or a doctor or a lawyer or a teacher or a film star or even, perhaps, a writer. Now those occasional youngsters who aspire to a career in writing need to be made aware of the excellent prospects for "with-authors." A "with-author" is someone who writes a book for someone else and is acknowledged by that someone else. It's the acknowledgement that separates the with-author (I now drop the quotation marks) from the ghost writer. With luck, the with-author's name will appear on the cover of the book that he or she has written. The type size will be somewhere between small and minuscule, but at least visible to the naked eye. Sometimes the with-author has to settle for being acknowledged in the book's preface. If the person who wrote the book is only thanked for contributing ideas, we are in the with-author/ghost writer gray area. If the person who wrote the book isn't thanked at all (except with a check), that person is a ghost writer, not a with-author. (Ghost writing is a noble profession, too, but let's stick to with-authors.)

With-authors make more money than ordinary authors. A hefty publisher's advance (at least part of which goes to the with-author) assures that the work will be published. As the number of celebrities grows—especially celebrities who can't or won't write—the need for with-authors grows. With-authorship is a promising twenty-first century career for those English majors who might otherwise end up as free-lance copy editors or waiters. As my own career illustrates, even a scientist can become a with-author.

Here are some of my recent favorites: *The Million Dollar Mermaid,* by Esther Williams with Digby Diehl; *A Spy for All Seasons: My Life in the CIA,* by Duane R. Claridge with Digby Diehl (yes, success breeds success in this field); *My American Journey,* by Colin Powell with Joseph E. Persico; *Journey to Justice,* by Johnnie L. Cochran, Jr. with Tim Rutten; *Without a Doubt,* by Marcia Clark with Tereso Carpenter (O. J. Simpson has been a gold mine for with-authors); *Work in Progress,* by

Michael Eisner with Tony Schwartz (business moguls are celebrities, too); and *The New Encyclopedia of Modern Bodybuilding,* by Arnold Schwarzenegger with Bill Dobbins.

Occasionally the with-author is promoted to the rank of "and-author." Consider *Yeager: An Autobiography,* by Chuck Yeager <u>and</u> Leo Janos. Pilots are a good and generous breed. Politicians, on the other hand, are likely to demote their with-authors to a bare mention in the preface, if not to ghost status. With-authors' names are nowhere to be found on the covers of recent books by George W. Bush and John McCain, even though the names of the books, *A Charge to Keep* and *Faith of My Fathers,* strike a high moral tone. (Nor does a with-author's name appear on the cover of Al Gore's *Earth in the Balance: Ecology and the Human Spirit*—but I dare not jump to the conclusion that Gore didn't write the book.) Bill Gates, an almost-politician, left the name of his with-author, Collins Hemingway, off the cover of his *Business @ the Speed of Thought,* but made it known to the booksellers, more than true politicians do.

When the putative author's input is marginal, we get into another gray area, that between autobiography and biography. Consider *Diana: Her True Story in Her Own Words* and *Monica's Story* (also in her own words), both <u>by</u> Andrew Morton.

But I digress. This is supposed to be an essay about my career as a with-author.

I didn't start out as a with-author. I fell into the profession late in life. In the fall of 1993, at age 67, when I was about to retire from the directorship of the American Institute of Physics, I happened to be talking to my old professor, colleague, and friend, John Wheeler (who was then 82). "Ken," he said, "I've just read Eugene Wigner's autobiography, and it inspires me to try to do something similar. But I know I can't do it alone. Can you suggest someone I might work with?" (Wigner, a Princeton professor and Nobel laureate, was a good friend of Wheeler. He was one of Hungary's many gifts to American science.)

"Well," I answered. "I do have one idea. How about Edwin Taylor?" Taylor came to my mind at once because I knew him to be an outstanding teacher and an accomplished writer. He and Wheeler had published a successful undergraduate textbook on relativity theory. He was about my age. "He's a physicist who writes well," I said. "You've worked together before. He might be the perfect teammate for this venture."

"Good suggestion," said Wheeler. "Would you be willing to proposition him?"

Of course it crossed my mind that, with my retirement pending, I might have suggested myself. Wheeler was perhaps hinting at that. There were two reasons why I didn't volunteer. First, I had a draft manuscript of a modern physics textbook in a file drawer. In retirement, I might finally polish it off. Second, I had no confidence at all that I could do the job that Wheeler needed to have done. Years earlier, I had written a small book on elementary particles for the general reader, but otherwise all my writing was technical—research papers and textbooks. Besides, I knew myself to be more of a "data person" than a "people person."

I tried to talk Edwin Taylor into the assignment. He said he had too many other things percolating. He liked the idea, but he didn't have the time.

"Why don't you do it, Ken?" he asked. "You would do a better job than I anyway."

I doubted that. But I began to ponder. I talked to Joanne. She said both the textbook and the Wheeler book sounded appealing, but I might be happier with the textbook. I talked to Spencer Weart, director of the History Center at the American Institute of Physics. "No question," he said. "Do the Wheeler project! It's a once-in-a-lifetime opportunity."

In truth, although the textbook had some momentum, it didn't command my great enthusiasm. It was no longer a book that the world "needed." And if one thing has characterized my life, it is taking on new challenges, trying things I haven't tried before. OK, I told myself, if Wheeler will have me, I'll try it. I went to him and explained Taylor's unavailability. "John," I said, "I've been thinking it over, and I'm willing to try to be your scribe if you're willing to have me."

Wheeler, in his characteristic way, said, "Ken, that would be marvelous. Let's do it."

That was December 1993. The final manuscript went to the publisher three and a half years later, in the spring of 1997. *Geons, Black Holes, and Quantum Foam: A Life in Physics,* by John Archibald Wheeler with Kenneth Ford, appeared in the summer of 1998. So, over a period of more than four years, I learned what it means to be a with-author. I never had a better time.

What happened from the time of our informal agreement until the book appeared? Oddly enough, the very first thing we talked about was my designation. Right away, I wanted to be a with-author. Wheeler *and* Ford would imply shared writing. Wheeler alone would imply that he wrote it himself or had it ghost-written. In my mind, Wheeler *with* Ford would correctly imply that I had been the writer on his behalf. Wheeler was agreeable to this designation. We drew up an agreement specifying equal sharing of income and stating that our names would appear on the cover with equal type size—consistent with Wheeler's always generous spirit when it comes to credit. In the end, four years later, I said to our editor, Drake McFeely, at W. W. Norton, "Drake, please adjust the type size to suit your marketing needs. Wheeler's name should be prominent."

"Thanks for understanding," he answered.

How did we wind up with W. W. Norton? Some years earlier, Wheeler had been contacted by the New York literary agent John Brockman, who specializes in scientist writers—not any old scientists, only scientists of the first rank. So we went to Brockman. He jumped at the opportunity to represent us (meaning to represent Wheeler) before he had even the barest outline on paper. He caught a train to Princeton the morning after we phoned him and we talked about the project over lunch. He coached us on how to prepare a proposal that he could present to publishers. So my writing started not with Chapter 1 but with the book proposal. After a few back-and-forth's, with Wheeler reviewing every draft, Brockman was satisfied with the proposal. He conducted what he called an auction. Several publishers were interested. A German publisher with an office in New York bid $85,000 for the book. W. W. Norton, a respected independent publisher in New York, bid $75,000. (Norton had published a successful trade book by Kip Thorne, like me a former Wheeler student.) On Brockman's recommendation, we accepted Norton's offer.

Now all that remained was to write a book. Wheeler and I must have spent at least three months just talking about the outline—what should we cover and how should we organize it? Wheeler has the same disconcerting habit as his old mentor Niels Bohr, always wanting to discuss and refine and reconsider, never wanting to call anything final. (That habit of Bohr had in fact cost Wheeler dearly; once Bohr delayed a joint paper so long that its most important results were derived and published first by someone else—someone who received the Nobel Prize for that work.) Having been an administrator and manager as well as a scientist, I was more inclined to want to make decisions and move forward. But all was amicable. Just as Wheeler never lost his total admiration for Bohr, I never lost mine for Wheeler. Besides being a scientific giant, he was a wonderfully likeable human being.

In the end, we decided to devote the first two chapters to Wheeler's work on nuclear fission, 1939 to 1945, then go back to his birth in 1911 and proceed chronologically to the present. We also had to decide the balance between his physics and his life. Wheeler at first visualized a life story in which science was only mentioned, not explained. I had several reasons for wanting to include explanations of his physics. For one reason, his life *was* his physics. John had only vague recollections of people's appearance and quirks of behavior. He had total recall of their physics. If I asked him about personal attributes of a former colleague, I was most likely to get a disquisition on an idea that person had had or the work they had done together.

For another reason (back to "data person" vs. "people person"), I felt more comfortable describing physics than describing people. I had had more practice doing that. And for a third reason, I thought that the book would sell better if it included a good deal of physics for the layman. Wheeler, over the course of his long life, had worked on some of the most exciting physics of the twentieth century, and had worked with nearly all of the century's leaders of theoretical physics in this and other countries. So, as the writing evolved, I found myself drafting chapters in which the story line went back and forth between the narrative of Wheeler's life and the tales of his physics.

I was honored to be working with Wheeler, but not awed. I made no effort to adopt the Germanic phraseology he affects in his own writing, being guided instead by my own stylistic muse. He accepted this.

Over the first few months of our collaboration—the same time in which we were discussing the book's structure—I taped about twenty-four hours of Wheeler's reminiscences. Then I taped interviews with his wife and his three children and with more than a dozen of his former students and colleagues. (A skilled transcriber in Austin, Texas, turned all of these tapes into transcripts on paper and computer disks.) I read many of Wheeler's published papers and sections of books he had written. At the Center for History of Physics in Maryland I studied relevant historical documents and collected photographs for use in the book. In Wheeler's beautifully organized archives at the American Philosophical Society in Philadelphia I gained access to his research notebooks and much of his correspondence. For those parts of his life in which I had been a participant, such as his work on the hydrogen bomb, I had my own recollections as well.

During the three years in which I gathered material and drafted the book, I was teaching physics half-time at Germantown Academy. This gave my life an ideal balance. The teaching did more than provide respite from the book. It improved the book. The students to whom I explained physics every day were not so different from the "general reader" whom we wanted to reach.

Every couple of weeks, I went to Wheeler's office at Princeton University or to his retirement home in Hightstown, New Jersey. He would read through whatever writing I brought while I sat there watching and taking notes. Sometimes he would recall some additional incidents or dictate a few sentences or a paragraph for me to type into my laptop. In his earlier years, Wheeler had often liked to work in an "interactive" mode, through the give and take of discussion. Now, in his later years, he could work no other way. The book got his attention only when I was there with him. I treasure those many hours. Wheeler's rummaging through the recesses of his mind for a particular memory or a particular turn of phrase could be agonizingly slow, but the results were worth the wait.

An agreeable feature of a memoir is that it doesn't need scholarly documentation to keep it afloat. Nevertheless, it needs fact checking. On what day of the week did January 16, 1939 fall? What was the last name of the lovely Miriam who worked one summer for Enrico Fermi? Where was Wolfgang Pauli working when he advanced the exclusion principle? At what time did the westbound Broadway Limited leave North Philadelphia in 1942? These and more than a hundred other questions needed answers. A perfect job for my daughter Caroline. She was willing and was indefatigable in tracking down bits of information. Yet—wouldn't you know—mistakes crept into the book, not because she erred, but because I forgot to ask her to check certain things. One reader, for instance, assured us that Erwin Schrödinger was even then rolling over in his grave because we called this Austrian a German. Unforgivable. Fortunately, sales justified two more printings, enabling us to take what alert readers sent us and correct our worst mistakes.

When the editor who had contracted for our book left W. W. Norton, the company's president, Drake McFeely, decided to appoint himself as her replacement. He is the exceptional publishing executive who likes to keep his hand in by editing a book or two each year. So we got the benefit of working with the boss, and the benefit of working with a company that is not owned by a larger company that, in turn, is owned by a megacompany.

Not long after the book's publication, I got a call from McFeely. "Ken," he said, "the Wheeler book will be reviewed in next Sunday's New York Times. It's a good review. You'll like it. I have an advance copy. I'll fax it to you and to John."

Indeed it was a good review, written by the Stanford physicist and historian Michael Riordan. What a thrill! I had already found my role as a with-author completely satisfying. I had not a shred of regret for the draft textbook in the file drawer. But the Sunday New York Times! For a mere academic, this was promotion to a celestial plane. Other reviews, all favorable, followed—in *Nature, Science, Physics Today, American Scientist, Scientific American, New Scientist,* and various newspapers.

But the biggest thrill was still to come. Norton entered our book in the science writing competition of the American Institute of Physics in the category of books written by scientists for a general audience on physics

John Wheeler and Ken, AIP Awards ceremony, fall 1999

or physics-related topics. Looking over the landscape of such books published in 1998, I thought we had at least an outside chance of winning. Then I learned that the competition covered not books published in 1998, but those published between June 1, 1998 and May 31, 1999. Oh, no! Brian Greene's outstanding book *The Elegant Universe,* extremely well reviewed and selling like a Jon Kraukauer adventure, had been published in the spring of 1999 (by W. W. Norton!). So much for our chances.

Then in the summer of 1999, I received an e-mail message from a physicist I knew in North Carolina, John Hubisz. His message, as nearly as I can recall it, was: "Ken, do you consider yourself a co-author of John Wheeler's autobiography? I need to know by tomorrow afternoon."

At once, I had two thoughts. First, this guy is probably a judge in the science writing competition, and the Wheeler book is in contention. Second, I am probably considered ineligible for the prize because I worked at the American Institute of Physics. How terrible, I thought. My previous affiliation might deny Wheeler the prize. This has to be handled with care.

Instead of responding by e-mail, I called up my friend. "Well, John" I said, "I don't know exactly how to answer your question. It's certainly Wheeler's book. I played the role of scribe and helped bring it into being, but it's his autobiography, it's his life and his physics."

"Ken, this is supposed to be confidential, but let me tell you why I asked. Wheeler's book has been selected for the AIP science writing prize and we need to know whether to award the prize to him alone or to you and him jointly."

I paused but a moment. "In that case, John, I guess it's fair to call me the co-author."

"I thought so," he said, "but I needed to check."

I let it stand. There seemed to be no reason to get into with-authorship, and-authorship, and so on. I was elated. At Hubisz's request, I waited the few days until we got the official notification before exchanging congratulations with Wheeler.

That fall, we were honored at a ceremony with appropriate short speeches, checks for both of us, and the promise of embossed Windsor chairs to be delivered to our homes. After the ceremony, Wheeler said to me, his eyes glistening, "This is so wonderful, Ken. I couldn't have done it without you."

"John," I said, smiling, with my hand on his shoulder, "I couldn't have done it without you."

Caroline, Adam, Nina, Jason, and Joanne, Valle Grande, New Mexico, 1968

Adam, Caroline, and Nina, Camel Rock, New Mexico, 1968

Near Santa Fe, New Mexico, 1968

Adam, Caroline, Nina, Jason, and Joanne, Three Rivers Petroglyph Site, Tularosa, New Mexico, 1968

Jason, Caroline, Nina, Joanne, Lucas, and Adam, en route cross country, summer 1971

Jason, Joanne, Ken, Adam, Lucas, Caroline, and Nina, Silver Spring, Maryland, Christmas 1982

GAINFUL EMPLOYMENT
Paid jobs

My parents believed that their children—or at least their male child—should work: not just doing household and yard chores, but doing jobs for pay. It wasn't that I or they needed the money. It was to build character. So I worked. And never with any sense of grievance. On the contrary, I enjoyed it, and was happy with the responsibility and with the extra money.

I had my first paid job in 1935, when I was nine. Every Saturday, for the few months that I held the job, the morning train that stopped in Reidsville, Georgia, brought me a heavy bundle of magazines. I transferred them to a burlap sack and sold them on a street corner. The market for *Saturday Evening Post, Ladies' Home Journal, Woman's Home Companion, Life,* and *Liberty* was strong. I also worked one day that summer picking cotton on the farm where we lived and was paid the going rate (per pound, not per hour).

Late that year, we moved to Ft. Thomas, Kentucky, where, over the next half dozen years (ages 9-15), I continued to be a magazine salesman (now delivering subscriptions to homes) and also did some yard work and babysitting. My family spent the whole summer of 1939, when I was 13, in a cabin on the West Branch of Grand Traverse Bay, just north of Traverse City, Michigan. I did a lot of swimming and hiking and reading that summer. It was there, on September 1, that the radio brought us news of the onset of World War II.

That was my last free summer until ten years later, when I was 23 and cycled around Europe. In between I worked two summers (ages 15 and 16) at a fishing resort on Lake Leelanau in Michigan; worked as a stockroom clerk at the Marine Biological Lab in Woods Hole, Massachusetts (age 18, while waiting for the Navy to call); spent two years in the Navy (ages 18-20); worked as a gofer at my father's construction company in Cleveland (age 20); and worked as

Ken, Princeton, New Jersey, 1952

a physics lab assistant at Adelphi University (age 22). Somewhere in there I also worked as a soda jerk at a drugstore in Shaker Heights, Ohio; as a clerk in a deli in Geneva-on-the-Lake, Ohio; and as a weed puller and all-purpose yard man at Pirl Beach, a Lake Erie resort where my family spent some summers. (Actually, that was one job I didn't much enjoy.)

As a grad student, I worked as a teaching assistant (1948-50, ages 22-24), then as a research associate at Los Alamos and back at Princeton (1950-52, ages 24-26). (see "Teaching") For that work I was paid the princely salary of about $5,000 per year, roughly what an assistant professor was paid at that time. That easily carried me through my dissertation year (1952-53, ages 26-27). Then my academic career was launched.

For the next 40 years (1953-93, age 27-67), I held a succession of jobs, starting in universities and ending at the American Institute of Physics. Along the way, I did some summer consulting at Los Alamos in New Mexico; and at aerospace companies in California—notably Lockheed, Convair, and Ford Aeronutronic. That consulting work was done mostly in the bloom of youth (1954-64, ages 28-38). I was also the beneficiary, in that period, of two fellowships, one that allowed me to spend 1955-56 (ages 29-30) in Göttingen, Germany; one that supported me in 1960-61 (ages 34-35) at Imperial College in London and MIT in Cambridge, Massachusetts. I think that my character was largely built before this 40-year stretch.

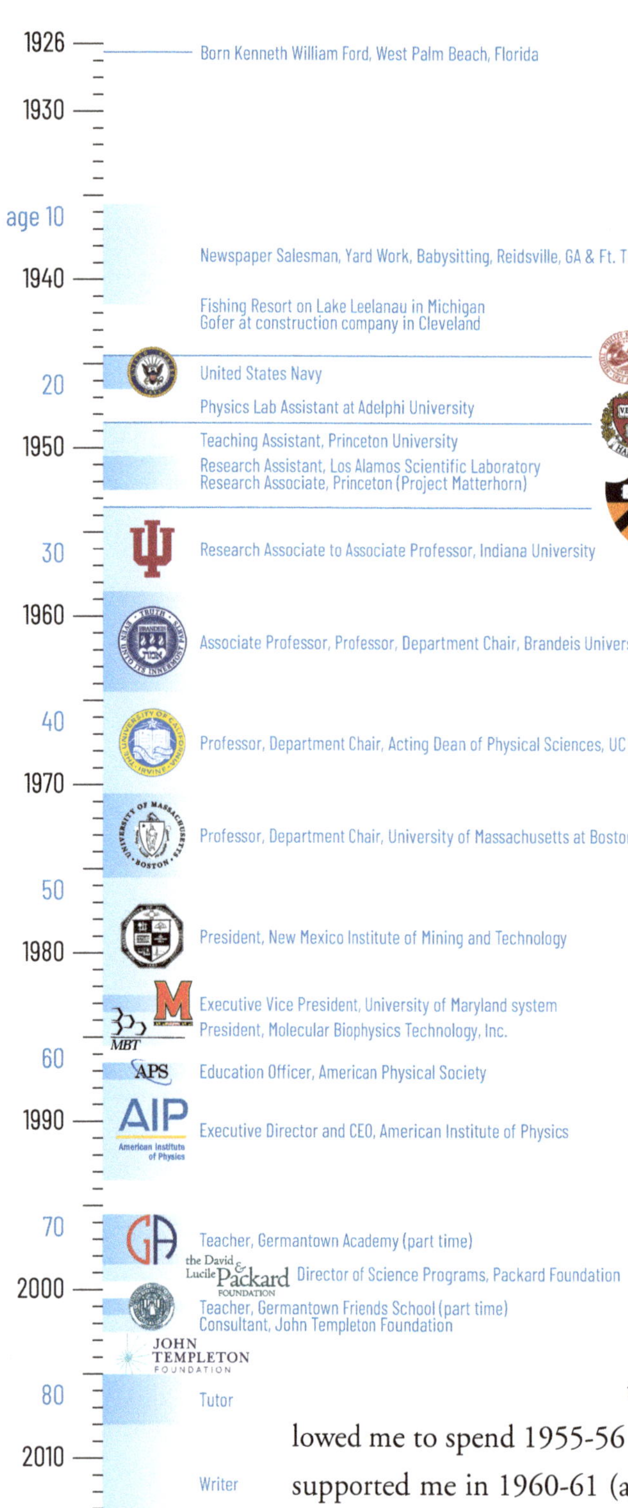

When I retired from AIP in 1993 at age 67, I was Medicare-ready but not rocking-chair-ready. Joanne and I agreed that something to occupy me outside the house might be in order. I knew that a university post was out of the question. I wondered if I might find a job as a high-school teacher. By a stroke of good luck I discovered an opening at Germantown Academy, within easy commuting range of our Philadelphia home, and found that GA was willing to take a chance on me. I had three very rewarding years there (1995-98, ages 69-72) as a half-time physics instructor, teaching AP physics to juniors and seniors and introductory physics to freshmen. I knew that high-school teaching would be very different from college teaching and hoped I could handle it. It was fun. I loved the students. It worked out well.

At this same time I re-engaged with John Wheeler, helping him write his autobiography (see "My Life as a With Author"), a job in parallel with the GA teaching. This required weekly or biweekly trips to Princeton as well as a few trips to Texas and elsewhere for interviews. The book was published in 1998, when John was 87 and I was 72 (in physics, that 15-year difference is called a generation).

The world of work did not seem to be through with me. In 1999 (age 73) I joined the David and Lucile Packard Foundation for a year as Director of Science Programs. This was a time when the Packard Foundation was upping its philanthropy and wanted to expand its science program. A very satisfying assignment.

Two more jobs lay ahead (not counting four books written and published between 2004 and 2015). One of these was a one-year part-time stint as a physics teacher at Germantown Friends School (2000-2001, ages 74-75). Again very rewarding.

Then, along about 2018, still casting about for a bit more of the gainful employment that had been baked into my being 83 years earlier, I found myself in a sidewalk conversation with a woman outside the High Point Café near where we lived in Philadelphia. She, it turned out, was a freelance copyeditor and got her referrals from the Editorial Freelance Association. When I showed interest, she said "Join." I joined. And I found that some clients were willing to take on this superannuated copy editor. So, as I write this, creeping up on 95, I can edit at whatever pace suits me. From the jobs I get some satisfaction and enough money to cover my Starbucks bills.

TEACHING
The greatest reward

As an undergraduate at Harvard, I was paid to tutor a varsity football player in calculus. He passed the course and retained his eligibility to play—my first teaching achievement. The summer following graduation, I found work helping to teach a physics lab course at Adelphi University on Long Island. (I lived that summer with my parents

Ken, Wayland, Massachusetts, 1964

in Garden City, a short walk from Adelphi.) Beginning in the fall, as a grad student at Princeton, I worked for two years as a teaching assistant, helping to oversee undergraduate physics labs. Those jobs at Adelphi and Princeton were, for me at the time, just "jobs," not a calling. (They were my last brush with experimental physics until I joined in a search for magnetic monopoles a dozen years later.)

My first solo responsibility for a course came at Indiana University. I joined the IU physics department in the fall of 1953 with the title Research Associate. This was a job that carried no teaching responsibility. But when I arrived, Emil Konopinski, the department's senior theorist, had a different idea. He said to me, "Ken, I am scheduled to teach a graduate course on mathematical physics this fall, but I am deep into research on the theory of beta decay right now and I want to devote full time to it. Would you be willing to teach the course?" Konopinski knew me from a previous summer in Los Alamos and must have thought that I could do the job. It didn't occur to me that I might not, in fact, be ready to teach such a course. I said "sure," and that fall, a dozen or so grad students and I learned mathematical physics together. A very agreeable experience.

I transitioned rather quickly to a faculty position at IU, and, over the next few years, taught courses at the graduate and advanced undergraduate levels. Student responses suggested that I was reasonably successful as a teacher, and I gained a great deal of personal satisfaction from it. It contributed to a balanced life—balance among teaching, research, and fun. During that time at Indiana, I also guided the doctoral dissertation work of two students, a different but important kind of teaching. And, during a year back at Los Alamos, I taught an evening extension course of the University of New Mexico on nuclear physics.

My first effort at teaching introductory physics came at Brandeis University. In my first year there, 1958-59, I taught graduate and advanced undergraduate courses, as I had at IU. Toward the end of that academic year, the department chair (I think it was Sam Schweber) came to me and said, half apologetically, "we all have to take our turn teaching Physical Science [the introductory course for nonscience students]. Would you be willing to do that next year?" Well, I thought, why not? It's a new challenge. That summer I bought several boxes of colored chalk and thought about how such a course should be organized. There were no strictures—no prescribed syllabus and no required textbook. Fortunately, it went well, as I designed my own course and made my way in uncharted territory.

At that time, representatives of textbook-publishing companies made their way among academic departments to promote their wares and to look for new authors. They were like pollinating bees, carrying news and gossip from one university to another. One such was a very personable young man named Yale Altman. I got to know him after he had left a post at MIT Press and joined a new company, Blaisdell Publishing (whose head, Warren Blaisdell, had himself left an established publisher, Addison-Wesley, to form his own company). During the academic year 1960-61, Yale, having heard of my physical science course at Brandeis, asked if I would consider writing a textbook for such a course. Being young, not yet fully aware of my limitations, and always open to new challenges, I agreed to do it without giving it a lot of thought. As it worked out, what came out of this agreement was first a modest-sized book for the general public, *The World of Elementary Particles* (see "94 D Cromwell Road"), published in 1963, and then a fat textbook, *Basic Physics,* published in 1968 (and a later offshoot, basic-physics.com). The fact that the textbook fell well short of best-seller status I "blamed" on the Brandeis students. As I wrote later, "I tailored the book for them [these students]: so bright and curious and articulate, and such accomplished readers."

At UC Irvine, the next stop on my academic odyssey, I continued to teach at all levels, and, better yet, I got to design the physics curriculum. At U Mass Boston, the next stop, I got special pleasure from teaching introductory physics to somewhat older urban students—most in their mid to late 20s, and many the first in their families to go to college. When, after Massachusetts, I landed in New Mexico as a college president, I con-

Ken, UC Irvine, California, 1965

tinued to do a little teaching. I was rewarded with this comment one day from a student after class: "Dr. Ford, you are a much better teacher than administrator. Why don't you resign the presidency and become a professor?" As the saying goes, he made my day.

In fact, to get back fully into the classroom, I had to wait for retirement. I was 67 when I retired from being the director of the American Institute of Physics (where I had done what I could to support physics education), and 69 when I took up high-school teaching. In those two years, Joanne, aware of my restlessness without a job, encouraged me to look around for a way to "get out of the house." I had the good fortune to be hired as a half-time physics teacher at Germantown Academy, an easy commute from our home in Philadelphia. I was well aware that success as a college teacher did not guarantee success as a high-school teacher—where lab teaching, not just blackboard teaching, would be required, and where lecturing would be minimal. In fact, it went well, and was, in some ways, even more satisfying than college teaching. When I retired from GA at 72, the school presented me with a lovely chair, something it didn't normally do for teachers who had served for only three years.

What next? After working with John Wheeler on his autobiography (see "On Being a With-Author"), and after a stint with the Packard Foundation, I found my way back into the

The English Department would be pleased if more students capable of succeeding in English chose to major in this subject, but, as you know, English is quite difficult. Only a small percentage of students exhibits aptitude for writing—the experimental part of our discipline—and talent in literary theory is even rarer. However, we had 5 English majors among last year's graduating class of 1,043. This is well above the national norm of 3 per 1,000. We are fortunate in being able to attract excellent students to our demanding program. Studies by the American Institute of English show that the supply and demand for professional writers and literary critics are now in balance in this country. It is not clear how our graduates would find meaningful professional employment if their numbers were to grow significantly.

classroom for a one-year job at Germantown Friends School, teaching physics to ninth-graders. There I celebrated my 75th birthday in the classroom. (For a few months that year, I also taught seventh-graders, stepping in to replace their regular teacher, who was out with a serious illness. What I mainly learned: Twelve-year-olds are not the same as fourteen-year-olds.)

My teaching was not yet at an end. Over the next 15 years, I tutored high-school students in my Philadelphia area in their homes and, working for a company called tutor.com, students nation-wide online. It was stimulating and enjoyable. But as I approached 90 and my brain's rpm fell farther and farther behind the rev rate of the teenagers I was tutoring, it became clear that it was time to stop. The work I now do, editing English-language papers written by Chinese scientists is, in its own way, teaching. So I guess you can say I am still at it.

In 2006, at the age of 79, I received the finest honor of my life, the Oersted Medal of the American Association of Physics Teachers, given for contributions to physics teaching. (It is named for Hans Christian Oersted, who, in 1820, made an important discovery in physics while lecturing to a class.) I titled my written response to the award "Love Them to Death." In it, I said, "At every level, I have loved the physics and the teaching and the students. Real affection for students, I suggest, goes a long way toward ensuring their success, and your own. When you really want them to share some of your excitement, they will."

Ken, SylvanDale Ranch, Colorado, 2003

COMMERCIAL AIR TRAVEL: TWO EPOCHS

Looking Out

TWA Lockheed L-1649 Constellation

I had reached the age of twenty-four before I first slipped the surly bonds of earth. One morning in July 1950, I climbed onto a TWA Lockheed Constellation in Albuquerque, New Mexico, and landed in Amarillo, Texas; Wichita, Kansas; and Kansas City, Missouri before reaching Chicago that afternoon. At each stop, I (and most of the other passengers) got off the plane and took in the scene—on the tarmac or in the small terminal building. Between stops, I sat glued to a window watching the land unroll beneath. I discovered that the one-mile-square sections into which most of the west is divided can be readily discerned from the air; they are set off by roads and fences and changes of crop. So, consulting the second hand on my watch, I timed our passage over the sections and calculated our speed. We were doing better than three hundred miles per hour.

Three years later, when I became a pilot myself, I discovered Sectional Charts, maps that show the land and towns and rivers and mountains more or less as they look from the air. Then, whenever I took a commercial flight, I added Sectional Charts to my briefcase, and kept track of our progress, finger on the map, eye to the window. When flight legs became longer and it was possible to fly nonstop from Albuquerque to Chicago, I still chose flights that made intermediate stops if I could, and I always opted for a window seat. As I watched the ground rise to meet the plane on each approach for a landing, I imagined myself in the cockpit. Down low, if I had the good luck to spot an optical glory—a bright ring of light around the airplane's shadow—I excitedly drew it to the attention of my seat-mate. Higher up, I looked for full-circle rainbows on clouds below. A friend of mine, Elizabeth Wood, wrote a book on experiencing science as an airplane passenger. I loved it. American Airlines printed extensive excerpts from her book in its on-board magazine. I wasn't the only passenger who looked out the window in those days.

Thanks to becoming a pilot, I visited, over the years, not just a few but hundreds of airports. Each had its own ambience, each its own special feeling. And at each it was worth keeping an ear cocked for the local accent or local locutions. (Once, when I stopped for gas at the Liberal, Kansas, airport, a woman serving me at the lunch counter said, in an accent that was almost Texan, "I love Liberal. It's the only place where you can have a snow storm and blowing dust at the same time." In Joplin, Missouri, I discovered that the accent of Gomer Pyle—the lead character, played by Jim Nabors, in a popular TV series of the 1960s—is real.)

Only once did I make it into the cockpit of a commercial airliner. On an Icelandic Airlines DC-8 flying from Reykjavik to Luxembourg City, I handed my pilot's license to a flight attendant and asked her to show it to the pilot and find out if I could come up front. She returned before long to say that the pilot would be happy to have me visit. I settled into the jump seat behind the pilot and watched as he and his co-pilot consulted their instruments and charts and talked to controllers. As we started down for a landing, I asked if I should return to the cabin. "No, no," said the pilot. "Stay where you are." So, at last, I did get a view of landing from the cockpit of a big airliner. The co-pilot handled the approach and landing. The pilot kept an eagle eye on the proceedings. Now and then, his finger meaningfully touched the airspeed indicator if the speed drifted the least bit from 148 knots, and once, with a hand gesture, he reminded the co-pilot that he should be turning right, not left. I suspect that my presence was a little intimidating to the co-pilot and that that was part of the pilot's intent. From my perch, the runway we were bearing down on looked awfully short, but the co-pilot made a good landing. I thanked the pilot.

Looking In

It's fifty-one years later. On a July morning in 2001, Masha and I walk through the jetway to board a United Airlines Boeing 757 in Philadelphia. Masha is my granddaughter. She is two-and-three-quarter years old. She holds one of my hands. In the other, I carry a bag containing crayons, coloring books, children's books to read, a blank tablet, snacks, and paper napkins. We find our seats near the back of the plane. Masha has a window seat. I am next to her in a middle seat. Next to me in the aisle seat is a man whose mien says "business traveler."

Masha had just spent two weeks with us at our summer home in northern Pennsylvania. She was learning to swim, and learning to ask, at the end of a meal, "May I be excused?" She loved to walk in the woods and she was faster than a hungry bear in spotting a raspberry or blueberry bush.

We settle in. I give her a snack without delay. Then books and tablet and crayons come out. As we drone on toward Denver, I spend some time reading to Masha, some time admiring her art work, and much time retrieving books, paper, and crayons from the floor. Masha doesn't look out the window, and neither do I.

I am feeling sleepy, so I ask Masha, "Would you like to take a nap?"

"No," she answers. She is full of energy. My eyelids droop, but I stay awake.

Masha is partially toilet trained but she is wearing diapers on this trip. "Do you need to go the bathroom?" I ask her.

"No" is her answer.

"Well, you tell me if you do."

She doesn't. We stay in our seats, and I continue to retrieve dropped items.

As we near Denver, I say to my other seat-mate. "I hope we haven't been too distracting."

"Not at all," he answers, and adds, "You're a saint." That startles me. I'm feeling only grandfatherly, not the least bit saintly. Do saints need naps, I wonder.

When we get to Denver, I ask Masha, "Do you need to be changed?"

"Yes," she says, "I do."

We walk hand and hand into the large men's room at the end of Concourse B. The changing table is at its far end, past a line of stalls on one side and a row of urinals on the other. Looking across from the changing table at a line of men's backs, Masha asks, "Are those the man toilets?"

"Yes," I answer, "those are the man toilets."

From Denver to Albuquerque, we again have a window and a middle seat. We have another snack. Masha busies herself with books and drawing, but she's getting restless as we get closer to her home. I sneak a look out the window at the Rockies below, whose higher peaks are still snow-capped. Many a time I've flown over, through, and around those mountains in a small plane. Looking down from twenty-seven thousand feet isn't the same. I turn my attention back to Masha.

CARS
More than 70 years of driving

My first car was a 1931 Packard Touring Sedan. I bought it from a Harvard classmate during graduation week in June 1948. I don't remember where I got the $300 to complete the transaction. Perhaps I had saved it. More likely I "borrowed" it from my mother, explaining to her that bargains like this don't come along very often.

Ken with his 1931 Packard, 1948

This car had a long snout out front, like the Cadillacs, Pierce Arrows, and La Salles of that era. Its two spare tires were nested on the two front fenders. Its canvas top stretched back over a rear seat, which had enough foot room for a wheeled liquor tray (or a bassinet). This top could be taken down or put up in as little as fifteen minutes after one got the hang of it. Its gearshift stalk was long and authoritative. Its cigarette lighter was on the end of a long cord that spooled out of the dashboard. The chauffeur (or I) could grasp the lighter, pull it out (which activated the electric current), stretch it over the right shoulder, where the plutocrat in the rear seat could grasp it, pull the cord farther, and light his cigar.

Changing a tire on the Packard would have been easier if I had first taken a course on the subject at a vocational school. Once, I drove two young ladies from Wellesley College to New York City, where they were bound for a friend's afternoon wedding. We had two blowouts on the way. I did not get them to the church on time. Their glee at my discomfort more than offset their disappointment at arriving late, and they were in excellent spirits.

I used and enjoyed the Packard for two years. Since I often drove it too fast around Princeton's streets after dark, I had the recurring fear that my claim to lasting fame might be as the driver who brought Albert Einstein's life to an abrupt end when he was out for an evening stroll. When, in June 1950, I was to depart Princeton for Los Alamos, I decided that the Packard was not the best car for the wild west. I chose my mother as my sales agent (she and my father then lived in Garden City on Long Island). I can't remember if I asked her to keep the proceeds of the sale. I hope I did. I do remember that we (or she) reclaimed the $300 it had cost and then some.

What *was* suitable for the wild west (and fit within my budget)? An Army surplus Chevrolet Carryall, at $400, seemed about right. It was really a delivery van with windows, three on each side. It had running boards; a flat floor in the rear, on which I placed a mattress; two side doors, one on the driver's side, one on the passenger's side; and a horizontally divided rear opening, half swinging up, and a tailgate swinging down. The chains that held the tail gate when it was open hung loose inside the vehicle when it was moving and clanged in a very satisfying way when the Carryall was driven around curves at just the right speed. I don't know in what year the Army took delivery of the vehicle. Probably in the early 1940s—early enough, in any case, that when I took possession of it, its engine had passed its warranted lifetime. Blue smoke poured from the exhaust pipe, and it needed a steady diet of oil. To address the problem I turned to a friend, Dave Nason, who had been an Exeter classmate and was, at this time, an engineer working for Texaco in Beacon, New York. He understood engines. I did not. In his garage in Beacon, we (mostly he) disassembled the engine, replaced its piston rings, and reassembled it. He was the surgeon, I the attending nurse. Presto. No slurping of oil, no blue smoke.

The Carryall took me to New Mexico and on many back-country outings during my year there. In June 1951, when it was time to return to Princeton, I got the odd impulse to go by motorcycle instead of car. I went down to Albuquerque, and bought a used BSA Bantam—150 cc, single-cylinder two-stroke engine, 4.5 hp, color mist green, capable of 50 mph. It afforded me a pleasant trip across the country via Colorado, Utah, Wyoming, Montana, North and South Dakota, and points east. I bought it for $325 and sold it in New York less than six months later for $225. Well worth it for the pleasure it provided. A friend drove the Carryall back to Princeton for me, and I used it for two more years, until, in 1953, it was time to return to Los Alamos. My grad-school roommate Ken Standing took the Carryall off my hands for $75, and drove off in it to his new job in Winnipeg, where it served him for a few more years. That final sales price reflected more the condition of the Carryall's body than my generosity of spirit to a friend. After I skidded into a parked truck on Princeton's Prospect Street on a snowy winter day, the car directed rain, snow,

cold air, or whatever the atmosphere harbored onto the knees of the front-seat passenger, with a commensurate effect on resale value.

I will not enumerate all the cars I have owned since then, nor try to explain why I bought and sold cars at such a rate. There always seemed to be a good reason. I stopped keeping records with car number 27 in 1992, shortly after I became Medicare-eligible (it was a 1988 Toyota Corolla). The number is by now north of 35,

The BSA Bantam on the road between Silverton and Ouray, Colorado, 1951

and includes Chevrolets, Pontiacs, Buicks, Fords, Plymouths, Saabs, Toyotas, Hondas, and Volkswagens (both bugs and buses), as well as the aforementioned Packard, a BMW, a Cadillac, a Volvo, and a Singer Roadster. As of this writing, I am driving a lemon-yellow 2017 Honda Fit with six-speed manual transmission. Joanne gets about in a 2018 Toyota Camry Hybrid. I am allowed to share its driving on trips.

1953 Plymouth, June 1953

I have not spent a fortune on cars because I have rarely bought a new one. I made an exception to the "always pre-owned" rule back in 1953 with car no. 5. It was a Plymouth sedan and cost $1,900. I had just earned my Ph.D. at Princeton, was signed on for a summer job at Los Alamos, and was to join the physics faculty at Indiana University in the fall. It was, in a way, a coming-of-age moment (I was 27). I bought a new car in the way that an 18-year-old headed for college might buy a new suit. By this action I was climbing aboard the "establishment" carousel. But almost immediately I fell off it. As I detail in my book *In Love with Flying,* I parted with the new Plymouth in Espanola, New Mexico after owning it for only a month or two, and used the proceeds, augmented by a little savings, to buy a much older Plymouth and an airplane, and hire an instructor to teach me how to fly the plane. (In case you don't rush right out to get the book, I must mention here that that action in the summer of 1953 launched me on very satisfying 50-year love affair with flying, during which I owned or co-owned six planes and rented many more.)

Another new purchase that I made was of a new VW bug at its factory in Wolfsburg, Germany, in 1961. I was on leave from Brandeis University, working at Imperial College in London (my mentor being Abdus Salam, later to win a Nobel Prize for his work on fundamental-particle physics). I ascertained that the savings resulting from factory pick-up—the price was $1,250—more than offset the train and ferry fare from London to Wolfsburg and the ferry fare back. The trip provided a nice break, in any case. The car was ceremoniously handed over with a few teaspoons of gas in its tank, and I was off for London. There was, at that time, plenty of free street parking within a short walk of my apartment in South Kensington (see "94D Cromwell Road"). At the end of my stay at Imperial College, the car and I boarded a ship for America. It was my main means of transportation for another year or two, during which time I married my wife Joanne, whom I had met in the summer of 1961, not long before I had departed for London. This is the only car that I ever sold for more than it cost me—in this case $1,350 vs. $1,250. That looks good on paper, but of course the car's "fare" from Southampton to New York was more than $100.

Another new car that I purchased was a BMW 1600 in 1968 in Costa Mesa, California. It was the bottom end of the BMW lineup, with a 1600-cc engine (thus its name), and cost $2,900. Since it was a BMW, I had to find out how fast it would go. I pushed it to 90 mph on the Santa Ana Freeway, and found it willing to go faster. But with State Troopers lurking behind every tree, I decided to settle for 90 as its verified top speed. It came to an ignominious end four years later on the Massachusetts Turnpike. I had to stop suddenly to avoid hitting a car ahead of me that had itself braked suddenly. Unfortunately the driver of the car behind me was less alert and the BMW ended its days crumpled fore and aft (it had been propelled into the stopped car in front). I was uninjured.

The third (1975) Volkswagen bus and the 1972 Volkswagen bug, with the H-BAR license plate

I must mention two other cars bought new, and one bought used.

In 1980, when my compensation as president of New Mexico Tech had reached the lofty sum of about $50,000 (plus a free home) and our family had leveled out at seven children, Joanne and I decided to go all out and buy a new station wagon. We surveyed possibilities in Albuquerque. A Toyota looked appealing, at $8,000. Or should we splurge and get a Volvo for $10,000? we asked ourselves. Yes, why not. So we picked up a bright yellow Volvo for a price we never imagined we would spend for a car, and with five of the children on board, headed to Colorado for a sightseeing and camping trip. For ten years, the Volvo served us well and escaped damage. In 1990 it made its way to the home of our son Paul in Oak Park, Illinois, where it was lovingly nursed through its elder years.

And now an epitaph to the memory of our beloved VW buses. We owned three of them and drove them across the country as well as locally in Massachusetts, California, and New Mexico. They were wonderfully roomy and fun to drive—although challenged by headwinds and hills. It seems that 50,000 miles was about the outer limit of life for a bus engine. Our last bus reached that milestone somewhere in Ohio or Indiana as we were headed, with a busful of children, from Massachusetts to New Mexico in 1979. We had planned to drop the eldest two, Paul and Sarah, in Bloomington, Indiana and proceed with the rest to Socorro. We were able to nurse it through its last miles into Bloomington. There, lacking other options, we traded it in on a used Dodge Aspen station wagon with, as the salesman explained, "cruise, air, and tilt" (cruise control, air conditioning, and a steering wheel that tilted). That got us all comfortably to Socorro, but we never fell in love with it. It yielded, after a year, to the yellow Volvo mentioned above.

Edith in the Singer Roadster in Garden City, New York, 1951

Much earlier, in 1951, having just returned to Princeton after a year in Los Alamos, I was overcome by the urge to be a two-car person. I had no wife and no children, and I had a little money in my pocket (my salary as a junior researcher on the H-bomb project was around $5,000, about the same as that of an assistant professor). My Carryall, or so I thought, needed a companion.

Genuine British sports cars were out of my range, but in New York I discovered that I could buy a new Singer Roadster (itself British) for $1,800. The deal was done. The Singer was a two-seat convertible, somewhat resembling the MG that was popular at that time. The Singer's horsepower was on the meager side, but the car's light weight allowed for brisk acceleration, and it cornered well. With the top down, the windshield could be folded forward to lie flat, giving the driver and passenger the illusion of being on a motorcycle, not in a car. It did lack a few amenities, such as a powered windshield wiper. When it rained, I had to turn a small crank at the top of the windshield back and forth if I wanted to see out.

My friend Dave Nason, the car-doctor who had successfully operated on my Carryall, actually did own an MG. When we made weekend trips together, it was, of course, in two cars. On one winter's day, in a large ice-covered parking lot near the top of Mount Equinox in Vermont, we competed to see who could cause his car to skid through the greater angle after building up a little speed and tramping on the brake pedal while briskly turning the steering wheel. I don't remember who won. Once, when I was speeding around winding roads on Long Island with a Wellesley friend on

Dave Nason tending to his MG with the Singer behind en route to Stowe, Vermont, winter of 1951-52

board, she cried out in delight, "faster, faster." She and I both survived into old age. The Singer was traded in on the afore-mentioned new Plymouth in Trenton as I shed the trappings of youth.

Ken, Karin and a VW bug
Goslar, Germany, October 1955

Before long came marriage and the need to be at least somewhat practical. When my wife, Karin, and I spent the 1955-56 year in Göttingen, Germany, we divested ourselves of my small airplane and the elderly Chevrolet that we drove around our then-hometown of Bloomington, Indiana. In Germany we found a nice VW bug that was only a few years old and was affordable (about $500). Among my young German colleagues, who traveled by bicycle and train, the car made me a wealthy American.

And finally, a 1948 Ford coupe that Karin and I drove from 1956 to 1960. After returning from our year in Germany in June 1956, and after a summer in Los Angeles where I was doing consulting work and where we drove a rental Chevrolet with its nascent fins looking ready to sprout, we wanted something "practical"—and affordable. My brother-in-law Joe Woodward had a young colleague who was getting married and wanted to shed her car. For $175 we acquired her car on Long Island and drove it to Bloomington, Indiana. It served us there for a year, then another year (1957-58) in Los Alamos.

That Ford coupe had two doors and a full back seat, although with limited leg room. Its rounded rear end resembled that of a rumble-seat car but covered only a large trunk, not outdoor seating. For the trip to Massachusetts with baby Paul in the summer of 1958 we found a suitably sized piece of plywood to cover the rear seat; it extended to touch the back of the front seat. Overlaid with a blanket, it was Paul's combined crib and playpen for about a week. When we arrived at our new home in Waltham, Paul was not the least bit interested in leaving the car for the house.

Time passed and took its toll on the now-beloved and now-aging car. Oil consumption, groans from the chassis, and loud clunking noises from the engine led finally to the diagnosis: inoperable. We nursed it to a suburban junkyard and accepted a $10 bill from the junkyard manager. We couldn't stay to see the beloved coupe violated. Karin burst out in tears and my eyes were moist.

Ken's 2017 Honda Fit with the customary H BAR lisence plate

MY LIFE WITH BITS AND BYTES

From William Keuffel and Herman Esser to Steve Jobs and Tim Cook

I acquired my first high-end slide rule in 1944. It may have been a present for my 18th birthday on May 1, or perhaps an Exeter graduation present six weeks later. I needed it—or, at any rate, I wanted it—because I was about to enter electronic-technician training in the Navy and was sure I should have the very best technology at my fingertips.

In 2016, seventy-two years later, my 90th birthday present was an Apple Watch. I needed it—or wanted it—to complement the electronic portion of our home décor, which, at that time, consisted of two MacBook Airs, two iPhones, and an Apple TV. Again, of course, I wanted the latest and best technology at my fingertips—or on my wrist.

The slide rule was a Keuffel and Esser (K&E) Log Log Duplex Decitrig, made of celluloid-coated mahogany and with a leather case. It cost $40 (close to $600 in 2020 dollars). I cleaned and adjusted it regularly. Some of my Navy pals and I competed with our respective slide rules to see who could get the most reliable three-figure accuracy in our calculations. I used that slide rule for about twenty-five years, and, for part of that time, another one just like it, which I bought so that I could keep one at home and one in my university office.

As a student at the University of Michigan in 1945-46, I took a lab course in spectroscopy that required calculating numbers to an accuracy beyond the capabilities of my slide rule, calculations that would now be child's play on a handheld calculator. The machine to do the job was called a pinwheel calculator. (Popular models at the time were the American-made Marchant,

Marchant pinwheel calculator

the Swedish-made Odhner, and the German-made Schubert. I don't know what model was in the Michigan lab.) It was made of metal, weighed probably around ten pounds, and sat on a table. It needed no electric cord. I became quite adept at pushing its levers and turning its cranks to make things happen. One could deal with numbers up to ten digits. What I especially remember is the satisfying routine for dividing one number by another. After entering the numerator and denominator, the user turned a crank backwards until a bell dinged, indicating one turn too many. This was corrected with one turn forward, after which the carriage was shifted to the neighboring decimal column and the crank was turned backward again. This went on, column by column, ding ding ding, until the result was achieved.

By the time I reached Los Alamos in 1950, manually operated pinwheel calculators were already obsolete. They had been replaced by electrically driven desk calculators, a few pounds lighter and much faster, but using the same logic, and also handling up to ten-digit numbers. I can't remember if I had a Marchant (or Monroe or Friden) calculator on my desk or if I had to turn to one of the "computresses" for help when my slide rule didn't suffice. The lab had one or two rooms full of these desktop calculators, all operated by young women. They followed instructions provided in rows and columns on paper, what now would be called spreadsheets. Enrico Fermi, a frequent visitor to the lab, used the "computresses" when he needed to, but also always had his five-inch slide rule handy. It was only half the length of mine but gave enough accuracy for most of his purposes and could be carried everywhere in a pocket. He was, in fact, famous for his attachment to this mode of calculating.

Also available in Los Alamos in 1950 were several IBM card-programmed calculators (CPCs), the newest and best at the time and the true predecessors of computers. They had "bodies" as large and heavy as refrigerators (or as IBM accounting machines, which is what they were), and "brains" with vacuum-tube electronics that were controlled, in part, by "plug boards." Input was by punched cards and output in long rows of printing on wide rolls of paper. The plug boards provided internal "programming" for calculating sines or cosines or square roots. The punched cards were read at the rate of a little more than one per second. If there was a momentary pause as a stack of cards was being read, it meant that the CPC was taking a deep breath in order to follow some plug-board instructions.

I was a rather heavy user of the Los Alamos CPCs in 1950-51. John Toll (another junior member of the theoretical team there) and I learned how to program the CPC and how to run it. Sometimes the runs stretched into hours or even through the night. Then someone else shepherded the operation. When demand outstripped supply in Los Alamos, I was dispatched to Sandia Lab in Albuquerque for a few days of around-the-clock runs on its CPCs. There I was accommodated in the BOQ (bachelor officer quarters). Although I was indeed a bachelor, I had never been an officer. Back in Princeton in June 1951, I continued using a CPC, this one in an IBM building in New York City. I was assigned the quiet shift—8:00 p.m. to 8:00 a.m.—and commuted from Princeton by train. (It was results obtained in these New York CPC runs in June 1951 that may have first convinced Robert Oppenheimer that the H-bomb design we were using would probably work.) Fortunately an all-night Hamburger Heaven was located just across the street from the IBM building.

SEAC, National Bureau of Standards, 1950

Computer development was explosive in the early 1950s. By mid-1951, the SEAC (Standards Eastern Automatic Computer) at the National Bureau of Standards in Washington was up and running and was, at least for a short time, probably the best computer in the world (the ENIAC was more famous but wasn't even close to the SEAC in its capabilities). By late in that year, the Atomic Energy Commission, on behalf of our Princeton Matterhorn team, had negotiated time on the SEAC (guess what time slot? 8:00 p.m. to 8:00 a.m.) I still remember what they paid for it—$20,000 per month (about ten times that in 2020 dollars). And guess who was to run it on this overnight shift? I found a room to rent in that part of Washington, hired a young man (with no computer experience, no physics knowledge, and no security clearance) to help, and went to work. John Toll and I learned how to program the SEAC. He and I and John Wheeler developed the equations we wanted to solve; John Toll and I did the programming. (Matterhorn was a project in Princeton, auxiliary to Los Alamos. Its controlled fusion branch, called Matterhorn S (S for Stellarator), was headed by Lyman Spitzer. Matterhorn B (B for bomb), which I joined in the late spring of 1951, was headed by John Wheeler. Spitzer and Wheeler were both Princeton professors.)

The SEAC had a clock speed of 1 MHz (a 2020 iPhone is more than a thousand times faster). It had about 3 kilobytes of memory (the iPhone has more than a million times that). It occupied two rooms, which could have comfortably held a few million iPhones. The SEAC had interesting "architecture" and interesting memory devices. It was called a four-address machine (a structure not mimicked by later computers). A line of code was like a clue in a treasure hunt. It might say: Take a number from register A and a number from register B; multiply them and send the product to register C; then go to register D to find the next instruction. Needless to say, we wrote out these instructions (several hundred of them) on lined sheets of paper, from where they were entered into the SEAC with a teletype machine. Their goal was to solve certain coupled differential equations.

The SEAC was outfitted with two memory banks, providing, as it were, a left and right brain. Either could be chosen by the flip of a switch, but they could not be used at the same time. The slower and more reliable memory bank consisted of mercury delay lines that looked like a set of fluorescent tubes. Within each tube acoustic signals propagated from one end to the other through mercury vapor, then got fed back electrically to repeat the trip. These were the bits. The faster and less reliable memory bank consisted of cathode ray tubes called Williams tubes. On the fluorescent face of each tube, spots activated by an electron beam were the bits. The computer "fathered" by John von Neumann at Princeton's Institute for Advanced Study used Williams tubes. Ours in Washington gave speedy but often irreproducible results, so I opted more often than not for the stodgier, more reliable mercury delay lines. Even with those, we had to repeat calculations to check accuracy. (See my book *Building the H Bomb*.)

In the fall of 1952, the single number that came out of all the calculations over many months was 7 megatons, the predicted energy release ("yield") of the Mike device, which was scheduled to be detonated on Eniwetok Atoll in the Marshall Islands on Nov. 1 (Oct. 31 in the U.S.). Its yield turned out to be 10.4 megatons. Given what I knew about the SEAC and all the approximations and shortcuts we had to introduce into the calculations, I found our 7-megaton prediction to be quite acceptable (even though John Wheeler said to me at the time, "Ken, we must have overlooked some energy-producing effect").

*   *   *   *   *

Post-SEAC, in the 1950s and beyond, big computers evolved explosively. I used some of them in my research, such as the IBM 650 (at Indiana University) and the IBM 701 and 704 (in Los Alamos), but mostly my contact with calculating and computing after 1952 was with desktops, laptops, and handhelds. One calculator I remember with special fondness is the Friden EC-130. It was a 42-pound monster, 24 inches stem to stern, that contained a long cathode-ray tube on whose face a "stack" of four numbers was displayed. It was the first fully transistorized desk calculator. It could add, subtract, multiply, and divide, and that's all. It used so-called reverse Polish mode (as did the first HP handhelds). A newly entered number was placed at the bottom of the stack and what had been the first, second, and third numbers were moved up a notch to become the second, third and fourth numbers. An arithmetic operation then acted on the bottom two numbers and the stack moved down a notch.

With my EC-130, I became quite adept at taking square roots by what is known as the Newton-Raphson method. You didn't ask for an explanation, but here is one, anyway. Let's say that you want to find the square root of 16 and have forgotten that it is 4. You guess 5 and divide 16 by 5 to get 3.2. Then you average 5 and 3.2 to get 4.1. Closer. Now divide 16 by 4.1 to get 3.902439024. Average this number and 4.1 to get 4.001219512. Still closer. Just one more round of dividing and averaging and you will get 4.000000186.

Friden EC-130 desktop calculator

Close enough. Take my word for it that this goes particularly quickly with stacked numbers and reverse Polish mode.

Hewlett Packard HP-35

When introduced in the mid-1960s, the EC-130 listed for $1200. I bought mine used for $600 (north of $4,000 in 2020 dollars). The seller must have known that this lovely calculator's days were numbered.

Indeed they were. Just a few years later, Hewlett Packard set off the hand-held calculator revolution with its HP-35. This marvel, with its wide variety of functions and its rechargeable battery, also used the reverse Polish mode with a stack of four numbers, but displayed only the bottom number in the stack in order to prolong battery life (the display used much more energy than the electronic heart of the device). It was first offered to the public in 1972, but I think I got mine a little before that. In 1971, as I recall, I was at a reception of some kind in Palo Alto, California, where Luis Alvarez, a physics professor at UC Berkeley and, as it happened, a member of the Board of HP, was also present. (Alvarez and I were fellow pilots, not just fellow physicists.) "Come over here," he said to me, "I've got something to show you." Standing aside from the crowd, he reached into an inside pocket in his suit jacket and pulled out a pre-release version of the HP-35, quickly showing me some of what it could do. I was enchanted. I had to have one. I can't now remember whether I was able to buy one or received it as a gift from Alvarez. In any case, I used it for many years and loved it.

When introduced, the HP-35 cost $395 (about $2,500 in 2020 dollars). Texas Instruments and other companies soon turned scientific calculators into mass-market products. A modern equivalent of the HP-35 costs no more than lattes for two at Starbucks (and is likely to be powered by ambient light or to have a battery that will last years).

*　*　*　*　*

This story has brought me only to 1971, a little more than 25 years since that first K&E slide rule and still 50 years short of 2021 and my 95th birthday. What has happened in that half century to computing and calculating—or, more exactly, to my computing and calculating? During all of those years, the power has been on my desktop, or accessible from my desktop, or in my pocket—one way or another, at my fingertips. Some of the things that have changed:

- where the computing power is—at a nearby central location (time sharing) or right at hand (a desktop computer) or around the globe (the world wide web)
- speed—from megahertz to gigahertz
- accessible memory—from kilobytes (SEAC and early calculators) to megabytes (early desktops) to gigabytes (recent desktops) to terabytes (the web)

At New Mexico Tech (late 1970s, early 1980s), a had a terminal on my desk connected to a campus computer—mostly so that I would feel a part of the modern world, not because I had a pressing need for it. However, I did use it, in conjunction with Lynn Orr, my fellow pilot, to schedule time on our jointly owned airplane. It also enabled me to write what might be called a surveying program, so that I could calculate the exact area of a piece of land just east of the Rio Grande that had been given as a gift to the school.

When I got to the University of Maryland in 1982, I arranged for a similar setup—a terminal on my desk connected to the HP mainframe that served university headquarters. My fellow administrators were puzzled. To them, a terminal on the desk was something used by secretaries for word processing. However, they soon followed my lead.

In Maryland, as in New Mexico, the terminal and the computer were only yards, or tens of yards, apart. Bridging hundreds of miles between terminal and computer had to await the availability of modems—which were not long in coming. In 1984, in Philadelphia, I acquired a true desktop computer, and, with it, a modem. The computer, a Kaypro, was portable—so-called because a strong adult could lift it. It had, if I remember correctly, 640 kilobytes of memory, which could be augmented by a 5-megabyte hard disk. Base price, $1,500; hard disk, $1,000. Total, $2,500 ($6,400 in 2020 dollars). I noticed, over the next two decades, that a basic desktop computer always cost about $1,500. Its power went up year after year, and, because of inflation, its real price went down. A welcome trend. A MacBook Air of the kind on which this essay is being typed is now available at a little less than $1,000.

The real thrill came that year in Philadelphia when I successfully linked the Kaypro, with the help of a 1200-baud modem, to a University of Maryland computer and saw the text, letter by letter, appearing on my screen at a comfortable reading rate. It was magical. 1200-baud means a maximum data transmission rate of 1200 bits per second. Before long, when I worked at the American Institute of Physics (1987-1993), we were using 2400- and then 9600-baud modems. The latter, which seemed blazingly fast at the time, are sluggish indeed by 2020 standards, when a full page with color can be transmitted in the blink of an eye.

I can't remember exactly when I got my first "laptop" (as opposed to "desktop") computer. It was probably around 1995. That laptop was an "IBM compatible" machine, meaning that its hardware was licensed from IBM and its operating software was provided by Microsoft. I used it in my teaching at Germantown Academy (1995-1998), in writing John Wheeler's autobiography (also 1995-1998), and in my work for the Packard Foundation (1998-1999). Soon thereafter I switched to Apple, and this essay is being written on a MacBook Air acquired in 2013.

Around 2015 I gave my old K&E slide rule to a grandson, showing him how to adjust it and explaining how some of its operations were based on logarithms (a major 19th century approach to calculating). Thus its name, Log Log Duplex Decitrig. He displayed only mild interest, then went back to his handheld calculator and his desktop computer. Yet a Web search reveals that there are now plenty of antiquarians out there who are collectors of things like K&E slide rules, pinwheel calculators, Friden electronic calculators, and HP-35's.

As I look back on my own 77-year love affair with what I will call mechanized arithmetic, it strikes me that the growth in digital storage capacity is even more remarkable than the growth in computing speed. Once kilobytes cost hundreds of kilodollars. I remember a later time when 5 megabytes cost $1,000. Now gigabytes are basically free. How can it be, I ask myself, that what we call social media (Facebook, Instagram, Twitter, etc.) allow their users, without cost (other than enduring ads), to post endless photos and videos? Most of this "posting" is over the air—i.e., transmitted by electromagnetic waves—less than a century and a half since Heinrich Hertz first transmitted an electromagnetic signal across a room. I am reminded of a cartoon in which a boy asks, "Dad, what's a wire?"

Ken with his iPhone, Philadelphia, Pennsylvania, May 7, 2016

ON WRITING: A LOOK BACK

A young writer's first book

This is a mystery story. The mystery is how I wrote as well as I did when I tackled my first book. As a writer, I was a complete beginner. I had not studied writing beyond a standard college English course. The only books I had read that dealt with the written word were I. A. Richards' *How to Read a Page* and Strunk and White's *Elements of Style* (which, in fact, I may have read later). I did almost no self-editing and no rewriting. And I was, at the time, doing other things besides writing.

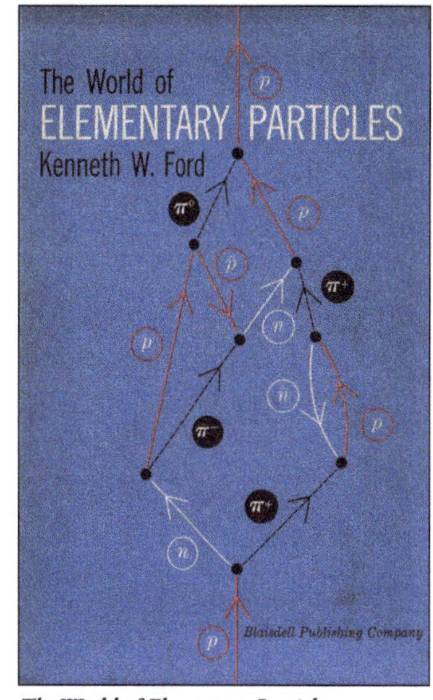

The World of Elementary Particles

It was September 1961. I was thirty-five years old and recently divorced. I had come to London to spend a year on a fellowship at Imperial College. I had brought two graduate students with me, and left two young children at home. The idea of a bed-sitter, as Londoners call a rented room, was not to my liking—just too lonely—so I opted for an available room in a large apartment already occupied by Michael, Mercedes (known as Mercy), Kathy, and Kathy's young daughter, Anna. It was a congenial group. We shared meals and made do with a single bathtub (see "94D Cromwell Road").

I had signed a contract to write a physics textbook, but found the prospect so daunting that I sought and got my publisher's blessing to try my hand first at a shorter book for a general audience. (The textbook, when it was finally published six years later, came to nearly 1,000 pages. The book I wrote in London in six months was one-fourth as long.)

I quickly established a pattern of activity. After breakfasting with my new friends and checking the first mail delivery, I walked to my office at Imperial College, studied, talked with my graduate students (who shared the office), exchanged ideas with other physicists over "elevenses" or over lunch, and tried to make some progress on my own research project. My mentor was the Pakistani physicist Abdus Salam (later to be the only Pakistani ever awarded a Nobel Prize). In the afternoon, I came home for tea, which merged into dinner. After we all talked for a while and got the dishes washed and put away, I migrated to my room to write letters and write a book. Sometimes, I would go to a movie or have my more musically inclined graduate student come by to play recorders. Even then, I tried to find some time for writing in the late evening.

Within a few days of my arrival, I had bought several pads of lined paper at a local stationer and written down, on a single sheet, a table of contents and brief notes on what should be in each chapter. Then, with my preferred fountain pen, I wrote page number 1 at the top of a blank sheet, and dived in:

> 1. The Elementary Particle Zoo
> When a jet plane passes by high overhead, the cloud of ice crystals formed in its trail is clearly visible even when the airplane itself cannot be seen. It is a piece of good luck for man that the smallest objects he knows anything about — the bits of matter and energy which ~~have come~~ are called elementary particles — behave in a similar way.

This paragraph shows a little editing, but not much—editing that was done on the fly, not later. Would I do it differently now? I would change "man" to "us researchers," "he knows" to "we know," and "which" to "that." Otherwise, I would leave it alone.

As I look back now at that hand-written manuscript, I am totally mystified at how well it reads and how little I edited it. The publisher did hardly any editing either, so it hit the streets pretty much as it got written in longhand.

Did I become more self-critical as the writing progressed? Apparently not. In 2007 I had a look at handwritten pages 468-469, probably written in December of that London fall. (Sometime around 2010, in the midst of housecleaning, I decided I just couldn't assign my carefully preserved first manuscript to the trash. I advertised it on eBay and found a buyer.) They are embarrassingly "clean," and include the following sentence:

> The new view of space was to be compared with a dry creek bed in the west instead of with the depths of a calm ocean; the new view of an electromagnetic wave, to be compared with a sudden spring freshet flowing down the creek bed instead of a wave of pressure traveling through the sea.

Not bad. I'd leave it alone.

I wonder if the weather and the lack of central heating had something to do with the flow of writing at this stage. As winter approached and London got frigid, I used an electric heater (what the British call an electric fire) to warm myself as I wrote. The heater directed its warmth in a fairly narrow beam, so if I leaned back to ponder, I lost its benefit. My electric fire may well have been a deterrent to more thoughtful self-editing.

I went back to America for Christmas and did no writing there, resuming the writing when I got back to London in January. With the manuscript almost finished, I went on a ski holiday to Wengen, Switzerland in February. There, in my hotel room, after each day of skiing and whatever conviviality followed in a local *apres-ski* hangout, I continued to write. When I ran out of ink, I finished the book in pencil, still with hardly any editing or re-writing. Here is a segment from pages 608-609, just after the ink-to-pencil transition (the book ends on page 611):

> In the seventeenth century man looked upward and outward into the universe and was humbled, as his earth took its diminutive place as a speck of matter in a corner of the cosmos. In this century we look downward and inward and find new reasons for humility.

Still acceptable, I think (except, of course, that "man" should be "humankind").

*   *   *   *   *

In the first chapter of his book *On Writing Well,* William Zinsser describes a Dr. Brock, who, despite breaking every rule of writing, was a successful author. I started my writing career as a Dr. Brock. That first book, written as if paper and ink were high-priced commodities, got good reviews, went through a number of printings, and found its way into Russian, German, and Italian translations. (It even won a science writing prize in Italy.) But how? Why? I don't pretend to understand.

As time went on, I left Dr. Brock behind. I continued to write with a fountain pen, but added scissors and Duco cement to my writing arsenal. Then more of what I wrote ended up in the waste basket (although I fell far short of the classic movie writer who tears sheet after sheet from the typewriter and litters the floor with crumpled pages).

Now, with the computer as a tool, I write, edit, rewrite, edit some more, rewrite some more, and then conclude that what I have produced could stand improvement. I have no doubt tinkered more with this little essay than with the whole of my first book. What does this mean? That my standards have risen? Maybe. That my writing has improved? I'm doubtful about that. That it's easier to write about physics than about oneself? Yes, for sure. That my brain has weakened? No doubt—although writing doesn't require a brain that is swift, only one that is more or less free of cobwebs.

So I leave the Mystery of the Young Writer unsolved.

Ken, Shunk, Pennsylvania, August 12, 2017

EPILOGUE

Thank you, dear reader, if you have made it this far, through the thicket of calculators, cars, and colleges; rebellion, regrets, and repetitions.

Thank you, dear children, for being so wonderful and for adding your own stupendous children to this world. Thank you, Joanne, for your tolerance, support, and love.

For this particular project, thanks to my sister Nancy Bunzli for providing photographs of me as a child. And thanks, above all, to my son Adam, who encouraged the project, acquired the photographs, coached his father, assembled the book, and saw it through the press.

Ken / Daddy / Pop

2021

Ken on Beechcraft Debonair, Socorro, New Mexico, 1978

Joanne and Ken, mid-70s

Ken and Joanne, Shunk, Pennsylvania, August 8, 2016

Images

Ken, climbing Truchas Peak, New Mexico, 1958

Ken, "climbing" the steps to the treehouse, Shunk, Pennsylvania, September 9, 2019

www.ingramcontent.com/pod-product-compliance
Lightning Source LLC
Chambersburg PA
CBHW041158300726
48981CB00004B/296